Realms of Wondrous Gifts

Also by the author

Santoshan with Swami Dharmananda

The House of Wisdom: Yoga Spirituality of the East and West, with a Foreword by Glyn Edwards

Santoshan with Glyn Edwards

Tune in to your Spiritual Potential

Unleash your Spiritual Power and Grow: Reflect and Learn to Trust the Power Within (previously titled *21 Steps to Reach your Spirit*)

Creation Centred Spiritualism: Merging the Intuitive with the Inclusive (forthcoming)

REALMS
OF WONDROUS
GIFTS

Psychic, Mediumistic and Miraculous Powers

in the Great Wisdom Traditions

SANTOSHAN

With conversations with

Glyn Edwards

THE
GORDON HIGGINSON
FELLOWSHIP

Published by
The Gordon Higginson Fellowship
1st Floor, Eastgate House
46 Wedgewood Street
Fairford Leys
Aylesbury
Buckinghamshire
HP19 7HL
(books cannot be ordered from the above address)
www.ghf-web.com
info@ghf-web.com
bookorders@ghf-web.com

ISBN 978-0-9557527-0-4

Design: Santoshan (Stephen Wollaston).
Printed by Sri Aurobindo Ashram Press, Pondicherry, India.
Cover photos: Santoshan by Tony Russell. Glyn Edwards by Santoshan.

Permission to use extracts from *The House of Wisdom: Yoga Spirituality
of the East and West* granted by O Books.

There is a sea of universal spirituality flowing through all the great wisdom traditions. All we need to do is immerse ourselves into the ocean of this knowledge in order to draw wholesome nourishment from it, and awaken to a deep and meaningful loving unity with all.

SANTOSHAN

Dedication
This book is dedicated to the spiritual heroes who have sought to cross all boundaries and establish peace in the world, and have encouraged a more caring attitude towards Mother Earth and all life upon her, and to those who have joined them in their quest and put their wisdom into practice.

Special Thanks
I wish to thank Graham Hewitt and Glyn Edwards for approaching me with the idea of writing this book and for encouraging me to expand upon a piece written for *The House of Wisdom: Yoga Spirituality of the East and West*. A special thanks also goes to O Books for allowing extracts of the original composition to be used and to Christine Linacre for kindly assisting with the proof reading.

Contents

ABBREVIATIONS

BCE	*Before the Common Era*
	(contemporary term for BC)
CE	*Common Era*
	(contemporary term for AD)
Cor.	*Corinthians*
Eph.	*Ephesians*
Exod.	*Exodus*
Heb.	*Hebrews*
Josh.	*Joshua*
Kgs.	*Kings*
Lev.	*Leviticus*
Matt.	*Matthew*

About the Author

Santoshan (Stephen Wollaston) has compiled, edited and co-authored three previous books on spiritual matters. He is the wisdom studies and creative adviser of the Gordon Higginson Fellowship for Integral Spirituality, and holds a degree in religious studies and a post graduate certificate in religious education from King's College London. He also studied graphic design at the London College of Printing and Psychosynthesis psychology and has a background as a musician.

His postgraduate studies focused on Critical Realist philosophy and holistic approaches in spiritual education. He prefers to have no labels, unless it be Integral Non-dualist or Creation Centred Universalist, and was given the name 'Santoshan' (contentment), by the respected yoga master Swami Dharmānanda Saraswati Maharaj.

Preface

This book emerged out of a short article, which focused primarily on Christian spirituality. In writing this book I aimed at presenting the evidence as it revealed itself. I was drawn to discovering the core of different views about psychic, mediumistic and miraculous powers, and wanted to investigate the variety of experience there is to be found in many of the great wisdom traditions. Obviously every writer brings their own thoughts and observations with them. However, I have aimed at allowing the teachings and voices of those who had something to say about certain experiences and gifts that can manifest on the mystical and spiritual path speak for themselves – whether 'for' or 'against' certain practices. In the first and final chapter and in places where the choice of who to draw upon for a contemporary perspective is where my own preference and reflections sometimes come through the loudest. I also feel that we can no longer talk about Christianity without considering some of the teachings of the Gnostic Gospels and have, therefore, included a few points they raise.

Knowing the contemporary intuitive Glyn Edwards (Devadasa) as a close friend also seemed like an

11

opportunity not to be missed to include him in this book, particularly as he was once a Christian contemplative, has studied the lives and teachings of many of the great masters of spirituality, and has his own perspectives on the powers. This was the reason for including two interviews with him for the Appendices, in which he eloquently answered some difficult questions and shared thoughts that I had not heard him talk about before. His universal beliefs are about a collective responsibility for each other and our planet, as we are a single family, eternally evolving in the one interconnected Spirit that seeks harmonious expression through all. In our multi-faith world, it is hoped that those who do not come from the same background as he has, will still, nonetheless, find much of what he had to say insightful.

Additionally, a glossary of terms linking with various areas that are looked at in this book has been included, to explain various key words students have asked me about during various talks I have given, in both schools and in the public arena. Readers will notice that this book does not focus on arguments about whether some accounts, such as popular legends about key individuals or miraculous happenings in the Christian and Hebrew Bible, should be considered factual or not; for it is moving into the area of personal belief and is the topic for another book, although I have offered alternative perspectives about matters for consideration in one or two places.

Introduction

There was a time when writing a book of this nature would have been considered as being out of touch with current thinking by the scientifically minded. The hypothesis put forward by James Frazer in *The Golden Bough*, published over a hundred years ago, was that humans have evolved from mythical indigenous beliefs in magic and in many spirits interrelated with nature, and tribal communities who respected the Earth's bio-diversity, to formalised religions influencing the structures of the great civilisations of history, to a scientific age and way of relating to life and the universe, which has no need for the beliefs and practices of the previous two stages.

For some, Frazer's path to cold scientific and dualistic logic holds the final view, and for many years mechanistic science was thought to have proven once and for all that life was nothing mysterious, and promoted ideas about nature needing to be controlled, dominated and paid little respect. A spirit world, or a sacred Earth to be celebrated, revered, cherished and lived in harmony with, or a cosmos with spiritual implications and purpose, were pushed aside in favour of theories about life and the planets being

13

nothing more than regulated machines, with no Creative Mind permeating and underlying them, and no room for such things as psychic, shamanistic and mediumistic phenomena, the miraculous, or ideas about the sacredness of existence.

Yet this is not the end of the story. For we currently live in exciting times, where some physicists and scientific philosophers, such as Joel Primack and Nancy Ellen Abrams, are discovering that humans hold a special place in a living universe which is not without significance. Some contemporary scientists are validating psychic phenomena and transcendent and spiritual realms of experience as fact, and have once again joined the search to discover what they imply and how we can best understand and awaken to diverse powers related to life – seeking how to responsibly manifest different abilities and live in harmony with the realms of nature and spirituality they connect with.

Similar to Carl Jung's collective unconscious, the studies and theory of the Cambridge biologist Rupert Sheldrake into morphogenetic fields (a biological field permeating nature, which contains information to shape the exact form of living things, as well as behaviour) point to an interconnected creative and psychic mind of the world and all life upon it. In John David Ebert's *Twilight of the Clockwork Gods*, he mentions how doctors, such as Richard Gerber, Larry Dossey and Deepak Chopra, are taking ancient microcosmologies seriously, as well as yogic beliefs about *kundalini* and *pranic* energy. A spirit world, a sacred Earth, telepathy, angels, reincarnation and the existence of the soul are all areas of earnest discussion for many respected contemporary scientists.

Ebert mentions how the Princeton Engineering Anomalies Research programme have meticulously documented the reality of paranormal phenomena, such as telepathy, psychokinesis and remote viewing. In the DVD version of the excellent *What the Bleep do We Know?* (extended English version), Dr Dean Radin, a senior scientist at the Institute of Noetic Sciences, mentions how it is no longer a case of asking whether scientists believe in psychic abilities or not, as many of them do. Contemporary terms, such as Precognitive Events, are now being employed by them to investigate a vast array of spiritual, mediumistic and psychic phenomena and wisdom.

With this in mind, let us look at some traditional myths, accounts, and documented comments and experiences of various yogis, mystics, seers and prophets and their teachings about them and search for a central core that might unite them all. But before we do this, I feel it is wise to reflect upon some areas that connect with the subject of this book – which are explored in the following chapter.

Ancient Wisdom, Postmodern World

> *There are different kinds of spiritual gifts, but they all come from the same Spirit.*
>
> CORINTHIANS

What are often classified as supernormal powers can be seen to connect with various forces of nature, such as having control over the weather or natural phenomena. They can also be seen to connect with prophecies about coming events, communicating with departed spirit personalities, numerous states and stages of meditation, ultimate levels of spiritual being and various types of healing. The word 'miracle' refers to an event that is invariably attributed to have happened through the intervention of a Divine agency or a higher spiritual force, and because of this, miracles are generally looked upon as beyond ordinary scientific explanation and not bound by nature's laws.

Over the last hundred years there has been a blurring of different types of spiritual, mediumistic and psychic experience. While it can at times be difficult to draw a clear line between where one type of experience ends and

17

another begins, it is a mistake I feel to reduce everything to a single category. One cap cannot usually be made to fit all.

I recently stumbled across an extensive pamphlet entitled *Psychic Influences in World Religions*, written with deep conviction by the Spiritualist James F Malcolm and noticed that he placed a variety of experiences, including mysticism, under the heading of mediumship. But if we look at what the word mediumship implies, we see that it generally refers to an ability to see, hear or feel spirit personalities that no longer have physical existence. Additionally, trance and physical mediumship and healers who are said to be aided by spirit personalities are other areas that can fall under this heading. The word literally refers to someone who is seen to be in the middle of two realms of existence – the physical world and the spirit world – and acts as a mediator between them. These two realms of experience that are often mentioned by mediums and shamans can be seen as quite different from the understanding of oneness, non-separateness and unity that is realised by many of the great mystics, where everything shares an interconnected underlying Divinity.

Mysticism itself, is about a life of prayer and/or meditation, reflection, work and spiritual discipline, dedicated to serving and discovering this unity with the Divine – found in all activities of life, yet also transcends all and in which all things possess an interactive relationship. While some mystics appear to display mediumistic types of experience or phenomena, Swami Abhayananda's enlightenment experience, which occurred in 1966, shows us that some do not and demonstrates how simply calling 'a mystic a medium' is misleading:

> ... I was not privy to the so-called 'subtle' realms of spirit; I saw nothing there of angels, spirit-guides, or souls. This does not imply that these do not exist ... My vision was one of identity with the Eternal, my original transcendent Source and ultimate being. I was able to see ... the outflux and influx of the universal cosmos ...

A blossoming of extraordinary gifts

When we look at the beginnings of a religion, we frequently find that there are reports of such things as profound meditational experiences, or we find a founder or an early leader displaying supernormal gifts. In the course of a religion's history, we invariably find holy men or women displaying various powers, such as healing and prophecy. Ancient scripture, such as the Old and New Testament, the *Yoga Sutra* and the *Bhagavata Purana*, mention a variety of phenomena that include the hearing of voices, visions, reading other people's minds and levitation. We hear about contemporary charismatic Christians speaking in tongues (technically termed glossolalia) and various mystics in all traditions performing extraordinary feats. Tibetan Buddhists have long-made use of oracles, who are said to go into trance states and become possessed by various deities.

One might argue that such things as oracles are

nothing to do with spirituality. But if spirituality is seen as a way of life and discipline, and oracles are being consulted as guides about various aspects of it, then they are obviously a part of it in some way. However, although this overview of five of the great wisdom traditions shows that certain types of psychic, mediumistic and/or miraculous powers can be found and practised within them, there is a general belief in not placing *too much* emphasis on them, which often comes through clearly as something that needs to be considered. For we must never look upon the parts as being greater than the whole.

Problems with miracles

With the subject of miracles there are ethical dilemmas and teachings which contradict the need for the display of supernatural powers. We are told in various teachings that if we wish to find a lasting peace we must at first accept things as they are. There is indeed great wisdom in this. Yet if we passively accept all things as they truly are, then the need for a miracle to occur to change anything would not arise.

In addition to this, people who have disabilities sometimes tell us that they are not looking for a miracle that makes them the same as everyone else, but would rather people just accepted them the way they are.

A positive change might be desired because of an inability to include all life. We, therefore, have to be careful that we are not using spirituality and various practices as a form of avoidance. There is also a tendency at times to want to jump in and quickly fix various difficulties people face, which can display this inability to embrace the whole. We of course need to endeavour to be there for others in a supportive role and exhibit spontaneous and natural acts of compassion, but the quick-fix remedy is not always a true display of empathy with others.

There are also problems when it comes to miracles not happening, as it could be interpreted that people's prayers are not being answered or that their practices are not effective, or even that they are meant to suffer in some way, which would seem like a harsh and unhumanitarian position to take. However, many miracles – if we wish to call them this – can be seen as not so much about changing physical circumstances, but in bringing about a pro-active acceptance of a situation. This kind of miracle does not physically favour people over others who might be less fortunate than them. An example of this is when suffering brings about a wholesome transformation in people's lives, which awakens them to connecting more with others.

Suffering can at times open the door to profound spiritual and mystical experiences, which help to bring about new and healthier states of being. But, as we know, this does not always happen, and there are no satisfactory answers as to why some people have these experiences in their darkest hours of need and yet others do not.

When it comes to healing we have to consider that medical science tells us that there are illnesses, even terminal ones, from which people can go into remission.

21

Additionally, there is also the placebo effect to bear in mind. None of this undermines the infinite possibilities of healing, but leads us to realise there is much we still do not know about the power of the mind and the body's ability to heal itself.

Synchronicity

Some scholars have looked for rational and scientific explanations for some of the Bible's miracles, such as what natural event might have caused the Red Sea to dry up just as Moses and the Israelites needed to cross it (Exod. 14:21-22), or could have changed the water of the Nile to the colour of blood, kill fish that lived in it and made it undrinkable (Exod, 7:17-18). Even if natural explanations are found for such phenomena, it is the way that the events are seen to happen at a certain time which gives them greater significance. Synchronistic events, therefore, can still be seen as miraculous happenings.

Drawing on Carl Jung's theory about them, some people have come to consider synchronistic events as having deep spiritual meaning, as illustrated in James Redfield's popular book and film *The Celestine Prophecy*.

Problems with experiences

Within all beliefs there are followers who want to claim the experiences and phenomena that unfold in their tradition show that their path holds the Final Truth, or that they have been chosen over others as special in some way. Some go as far to condemn anyone displaying supernatural powers, or having deep spiritual experiences, outside of their tradition as false. Or even worse, that they are being mislead.

In Carl Jung's autobiography, he reminds us that concepts are often built around experiences, which can lose much of what they are about. Deepak Chopra tells us that, "Finding the truth is not a matter of making anyone wrong, but of seeing how every belief can be expanded". But no matter what experiences are encountered on the spiritual journey, they need to lead to an opening up to the transforming influence of the Divine that is within, transcends and unites all.

In today's world we can take routes that do not rely on religious dogmas, but can still fall into familiar traps, as we might believe our experiences or practices give us the ultimate perspective on spirituality, the spirit world or life-after-death. Problems arise when the whole of development is overlooked in place of only one or two facets, such as only considering the philosophic and theological aspects of a belief system, or just the traditional realms of mystical and psychic experiences, though in the ultimate sense, all facets become part of mystical experience when the spiritual life is lived to its full.

Wholism, on the other hand, implies bringing *all part*s together in order to discover a balance and harmony of the many facets of life. For the majority of the great mystics, lamas and yogis, study, the development of the mind, everyday life, work and practices of prayer and meditation are unifying facets of the whole of spirituality. It is not a life of escapism and blissing out, but spiritually living and

23

acting in the world and using *all* our powers for good.

Deeper mysteries

When thinking about the views some have against psychic, shamanistic, mediumistic and miraculous powers, one question that keeps coming to mind is, 'Doesn't wholeness and oneness include everything?' After all, the New Testament tells us that God is in all (Eph. 4:6).

Obviously there is more to the great wisdom traditions than just wholeness and oneness. However, it can be said that they are important elements that link with them. For instance, the word 'yoga' comes from the verbal root *yuj*, meaning to bind and make whole. In a talk given at the Christian Meditation Centre in London by the highly respected Benedictine monk, Father Lawrence Freeman, he described the word 'holiness' as being a comparable word to 'wholeness'. In the Bible, holiness is about overcoming separateness from the Divine. So it seems that both words – yoga and holiness – imply a similar thing, which suggest an inclusion and integration of the many facets of our being. Further to this, the mystical strand running through various traditions invariably includes a realm of unitive consciousness experienced when we are fully present with all things, which overcomes restrictions of separate individual awareness (our limited sense of 'I', self or ego).

The Buddha's teachings, though we cannot technically talk about them as 'mystical' (as a mystic is someone who follows a path grounded in the Divine/God, which the

Buddha did not teach), they are also about realising an ultimate state of non-separateness.

We can, therefore, conclude that many of the great wisdom traditions appear to share some similarities in the different terms they use. And if all is interconnected and part of a Greater Whole, then it must imply such things as psychic, mediumistic and miraculous powers are facets of this reality. It would be odd to leave something out and to call it 'whole' otherwise. Although from a supreme perspective some may teach about a transcendence of all things, this transcendence, if looked at in a healthy and practical way, need not imply denying any parts. It can be about 'including and transcending'.

However, there is one area that does not fit so neatly with this view, as there are various ascetics in many traditions, who have renounced the world and all contact with it – which is hardly about inclusiveness – though accounts of such people often mention them possessing and displaying a variety of supernatural powers.

But it should be mentioned that completely renouncing the world is rarely practiced or even favoured. It was not the path of the first guru of the Sikh faith (Guru Nanak), the Buddha (although he tried ascetic practices at first, he felt they did not lead to enlightenment), Jesus, Moses or the Prophet Muhammad. The central message of one of Hinduism's most revered holy books, the *Bhagavad Gita,* is about involvement in the world, rather than escaping from it and puts forward a belief in ascetic practices not achieving their aim.

Problems with language

In writing about such a vast topic as psychic, mediumistic and miraculous powers in some of the world's great wisdom traditions, it soon becomes clear that there are problems with terminology and the way these powers are considered; for what might be classed as an extrasensory faculty by some might be seen as a miraculous gift by others.

We also need to take into consideration that any practice, such as prayer or meditation, which is believed to have a result or effect in some way, is basically a belief in psychic or miraculous power. Even if there is a psychological or physiological explanation for what happens, such as feeling more relaxed after calming one's breath. If an individual holds a belief in a power that brings about a transformation, it implies a belief in a psychic or miraculous force that can interact with one's life and bring about positive change. For instance, when bread is consecrated by a Roman Catholic priest during Mass and it is believed to transform into the body of Christ, it obviously implies a belief in a miraculous power.

To complicate matters further, we could consider, as Carl Jung did, that we can know nothing of life if it were not for our psychic senses, as everything can be seen as being perceived by and processed through them. For ultimately we experience everything as a psychic image in one way or another, i.e. in symbolic form, which has symbolic meaning to us, including language and all other sensory data. Visualisation practices can, for instance, be viewed as a way of entering into and working with the deeper psychic levels of our being.

Whatever conclusion one wishes to make, it is clear that psychic or miraculous gifts, although some might argue are not essential to spiritual and mystical life are, as will be seen in the examples given in this book, intrinsically bound-up with and frequently by-products of it. It is only when we do not heed the general warning given about over attachment to them, and allow them to distract us from other realms of development and use them purely for self-promotion that they become obstacles to spiritual living. For the path is multifaceted. Everyone is uniquely different with an infinite variety of gifts to share – which *does not imply* an I am more important than anyone else egocentricness:

> ... *your light must shine in the sight of all, so that, seeing your good works, they may give praise to your parent-God in heaven.*

MATTHEW'S GOSPEL

Exploring some familiar and contemporary themes

As mentioned, there are some that claim such things as mediumship and shamanism should not be practised. Popular passages for such believers are found in the Old Testament – particularly sections of Deuteronomy. Yet even Jesus is reported to have consulted with the departed Moses and Elijah (Matt. 17:3 and Luke 9:30). Deuteronomy fails to mention that psychic and mediumistic types of abilities have been known to surface naturally within people's spiritual growth, even when they have not consciously been trying to develop them – as fellow author of *The House of Wisdom*, Swami Dharmananda, discovered to her surprise when undertaking various yoga practices – or what people are meant to do if this happens.

The reason for one of the warnings given in Deuteronomy is because it will make us ritually unclean if we associate with certain people (19:31). This goes against any wholesome ideas of a spiritual inclusiveness and contrasts strongly with other passages in the Old Testament that remind us to "love our neighbour as our self" (Lev. 19:18), which the Jewish people are called to live and Jesus advocated as the second greatest commandment, after loving God with all one's heart, mind and soul (Matt. 22:37-39). The combining of these two teachings has been called the 'Jesus Creed' by some Christians, such as Scot McKnight, which amends the ancient Jewish *Shema*/Creed.

Other warnings in Deuteronomy are about divination, sorcery and witchcraft (18:10-12), of which the latter has links in various cultures with Paganistic beliefs, that are often about honouring the Divine Feminine and being at one with Nature and the Earth, which in today's world – particularly because of global warming – are important practices. Ignoring an Earth-centred spirituality and a Creative empowered Divinity, and Its interactive relationship with the universe, is looked upon as a serious mistake by many contemporary pioneers of spirituality, such as Thomas Berry and Matthew Fox, and is seen as a contributory factor that has caused humankind to not caring enough about global issues.

The witch that Saul is described visiting in the Old Testament's First Book of Samuel, who makes contact with the deceased spirit of Samuel, reminds him how he had expelled people such as her from the land, which shows a harsh form of persecution that would be unacceptable to any human rights believer.

On the whole, fundamentalist strands of any tradition will want to read holy scripture as a word for word factual document that needs little or no interpretation. Yet there is a problem with this, as there are invariably contradictory and ambiguous teachings in all the world's great wisdom traditions, as well as plenty of symbolic and metaphorical language used, and perspectives on life that are no longer valid. This means that the teachings will require personal reflection to arrive at one's own understanding and insights in order to make sense of the teachings. The cultivation of wisdom and personal reflection are highly prized in all healthy spiritual practices.

We need to remember that one person's truth can mean little to someone from another faith and that ancient teachings were given in times that were different from the world in which we live – even thirty year old studies on psychic, mediumistic and miraculous powers in world religions will be out of touch with contemporary thinking. Hopefully we would not put someone to death for working on the Sabbath (Exod. 35:2), as it is not only barbaric, but fails to see that every day is holy and work is a part of the spiritual life. Teachings from other eras and traditions, remind us that good works and wholesome and skilful actions are essential for balanced living.

The societies in which the historical Buddha, the first prophets and many of the early mystics grew up in cannot be compared completely with ours. The world in which we live is even vastly different from the one our parents grew up in when they were our age, and our understanding of science, spirituality, religion and the universe has changed. Having an 'I am right and you are wrong' intolerance will only create problems in our pluralistic contemporary multi-cultural and multi-faith world.

Noticeable changes in thinking and understanding

Many contemporary scientists and influential thinkers are bringing about changes in our understanding of the various powers we posses and how they relate to underlying forces at work throughout the universe. Scientists, for example, are discovering things that were once looked upon as supernatural – such as precognition – as being perfectly natural phenomena that connect us with all life, as they are bound-up with an interactive consciousness underlying everything. In contrast to this we find some attitudes of thirty years ago were not so open. Although taking an opposite view himself, Frits Staal pointed out in his excellent book *Exploring Mysticism*, published in 1975, that, "In modern scholarly literature such powers are frowned upon, and it is generally suggested that Patanjali [the compiler of the influential *Yoga Sutra*] himself also looked down on them".

Even in early Buddhism, the beginning of section eleven of the *Kevavaddha Sutta* of the *Digha Nikaya* mentions the exercise of supernormal powers, in which the Buddha condemns as vulgar conjuring tricks. According to the relatively recent *Rider Encyclopedia of Eastern Philosophy*, all the great masters have cautioned against psychic and miraculous powers because they, "belong entirely to the phenomenal realm and contribute nothing to one's realization of absolute truth, and because attachment to such abilities constitutes a serious obstacle in the way to spiritual development".

Various yogis, such as the 20th century teacher Gopi Krishna, warned against using miraculous powers and stated that, "Not one of the great modern Indian saints and sages such as Sri Ramakrishna, Maharshi Ramana, Sri Aurobindo, Swami Dayananda, or Swami Sivananda, endorsed the exhibition of psychic gifts or the working of miracles, even if endowed with such powers".

Yet we find Sri Aurobindo writing extensively about our psychic being and experiences attainable in dreams and meditation. He even experimented with automatic writing after his brother introduced him to it and produced various amounts of teachings through the practice, where what appeared to be a discarnate spirit personality wrote about different spiritual topics. Sri Aurobindo even produced the short book *Yoga Sadhana* by the method, at the rate of one chapter a day and completed it in roughly seven to eight days. Interestingly, in *Volume Two* of his diaries, he came to the conclusion that the writings were, "not always of a higher order", and according to his experience, he felt that the majority – but not all – "of such writings comes from a dramatising element of the subconscious mind". In a balance to this comment, we could consider the highly popular channelled book *A Course in Miracles* and conclude that the quality of such phenomena cannot always be dismissed so easily.

But no matter what the phenomena, we need to reflect upon their validity. Our own wisdom needs to play a part. The phenomena should not override the importance of compassionate actions, or the promotion of unity and peace with others, and living skilfully and wisely in every moment. This requires a deep ecumenical approach to spirituality, which wholesomely accepts that we do not have all the answers and respects the spiritual teachings of others. I use the word 'spiritual' here to imply teachings and practices that unite instead of divide people and their shared responsibilities for each other and all life on Mother Earth.

Yogis & Buddhas

The powers in Hindu spirituality

Yogis and yoginis tell us that astral beings are everywhere.
To know this truth, they must possess clairvoyant and
other types of shamanistic and mediumistic abilities.
When we look at the yogic and Hindu spiritual tradition
we find that since early Vedic times, around the 2nd
millennium BCE, there has been the belief in various
extraordinary powers, including the power of specialised
rituals and the creative use of prayer and mantra helping to
maintain cosmic order (called *rita* in Sanskrit). Some have
speculated that these rituals and the belief in their results
point towards an early understanding of creative karmic
action having a positive effect.

Within the Hindu tradition there is also the belief in
what is called *tapas*, which literally means 'heat'. This goes
back to the early *Rig Veda*, the oldest collections of sacred
teachings within the tradition. *Tapas* reflects the Vedic idea
of the God-force (Brahman), which is seen to reside in
mantras and prayers and is released when recited during
special rituals.

The generation of this mystical heat within oneself is

also thought to yield supernatural powers (called *siddhis* in the yogic tradition, which roughly translates as 'perfect abilities', and were also called *prabhava* in early teachings). For instance, through fasting or other disciplines, a yogi or yogini can build internally the mystical heat of *tapas,* which unfolds psychic abilities. In the later Epic literature of the Hindu tradition (*Mahabharata* and *Ramayana*), *tapas* refers to the practice of asceticism and its results, and as a power that can be transferred from a guru to a disciple. Here it is seen as a potent psychic force that is given to another in order to help him or her open up to numerous subtle levels of being and move forward on the path to enlightenment. There are various classic legends that mention some of the abilities of different yoga ascetics, such as the ancient story about how, through *tapas*, a yogi named Bhagiratta urged God to release the river Ganges to flow on Earth, which was said to have originally only flowed in heaven:

> *Bhagiratta kept his arms raised for a thousand years and stood on one leg for another thousand. When the Gods at last granted his request, the force of the water came pouring down . . .*

FRITS STAAL

The Divine being Krishna, who imparts profound teachings on yoga to the warrior prince Arjuna on the eve of a great battle in the *Bhagavad Gita*, is renowned for various miracles and heroic deeds in numerous legends about him. He is not mentioned in the early Vedic teachings, but has become one of the most revered figures in the Hindu tradition. Some scholars, such as my previous university lecturer, Professor Friedhelm Hardy, thought he must have been an actual historical teacher who gained a following in order to appear suddenly on the scene and be written about with such devotion.

There are scores of legends about Krishna in the *Bhagavata Purana*, which describe him defeating numerous mythical beings and creatures. As a child his adoptive mother Yashoda is said to have found the whole universe inside of his mouth and as an adult he is said to have stopped the course of the sun, so as to influence the outcome of a battle. He is also reported to have saved his village from the destruction of a giant snake by dancing on its head.

Powers of various kinds, performed by different teachers and masters, are mentioned in an array of revered teachings, such as clairvoyance, telepathy, making oneself and objects invisible, and the ability to leave the physical body at will and enter another body – even a dead body. In Swami Rama's autobiography he mentions a yogi that is said to have done this in modern times. This ability, which is described in the *Mahabharata* (*Anusasanaparvan*, 13:40-41) – the longest poem in the world, with many key teachings on desires, personal duty and spiritual liberation – is looked upon as a special power obtained by yogis and yoginis, and is thought to be a side effect of overcoming attachment and bondage to the physical body and worldly experience.

Book three of the classic *Yoga Sutra* teaches about various powers that can be developed through yoga practices. Once the practitioner has control over his or her consciousness he or she reaches a particular stage of meditation where certain powers are acquired, such as memory of previous existences, and knowing the cries of all creatures and the mental states of all people. These powers are the same as the superknowledges in Buddhism and are important features in both the *Yoga Sutra* and Buddhism for attaining liberation and spiritual freedom.

In the popular devotional text, the *Bhagavata Purana*, it describes the powers in detail, and states that there are eighteen of them in all, whereas in contrast to this, the *Yoga Sutra* lists as many as thirty. Yet where they are acquired through one's own efforts in the *Yoga Sutra*, they are tied up with the notion of grace in the *Bhagavata Purana* and are given as a blessing to the devotee by God: *Bhagavan*, the Lord of all *siddhis*. The power of omniscience, all-knowing, it is said, comes to those whose minds are purified by devotion and know how to meditate on the Divine Lord. All powers are seen to already exist in an infinite variety of forms in the Divine and are given depending on the devotees degree of dedication.

In the *Bhagavata Purana*, powers, such as merging one's consciousness with another's, entering another's body, dying at will, changing oneself into different physical forms, as well as ultimate liberation itself, are all achieved by meditating on a particular aspect of the Divine. Knowledge of other people's minds, for instance, is said to unfold by meditating on ideas. However, knowledge of previous births is not mentioned in the teachings. As well as this, the *Bhagavata Purana* does not grade the powers, because they are tied up with corresponding aspects of God – grading them would imply that there are higher and lower aspects to the Divine, which would be unacceptable to the teachers of the *Bhagavata Purana*.

The *Yoga Sutra*, on the other hand, makes a distinction between major and minor powers. The most important being linked with the final stage of liberation, namely insight into the difference between *sattvic*/pure-intellect and ultimate knowledge of one's authentic Self/*Purusha*. Having insight into the Ultimate Reality of all things is looked upon as the highest gift in all mystic traditions – each having their own unique understanding about its spiritual implications.

Connected with the more ascetic branches of Hindu spirituality are the Nath yogis, who owe much to Tantric yoga beliefs and practices:

> *The Naths or yogic 'Masters' are nine great adapts, of whom Siva himself is the first, parallel to the eighty-four immortal Siddhas of tantric Buddhism.... it was through the Nath Yogins that tantric ideas and vocabulary became current among the masses between the twelfth and fifteenth centuries.*
>
> J. L. BROCKINGTON

What is said to distinguish the Naths from ordinary yoga

37

practitioners is their power of control over death and decay. They were credited to have had extensive occult powers, which earned them a reputation as miracle-workers.

Looking at Tantra and Kundalini yoga, we find a variety of practices being adopted to awaken what is described as the latent serpent/creative (*kundalini*) psychic power at the base of the spine and raise it through various channels (*nadis*) and energy points (*chakras*) to reunite with *sahasrara* (described as the thousand petalled lotus) at the crown of the head. It is said that when one is able to do this, one experiences the reunion of one's individualised and universal cosmic nature (Shakti, the creative female energy) with the transcendent power of Shiva (symbolically seen as an unchanging male force standing outside time and causality); neither of which are in fact seen as being superior to, or separate from, the other in Tantra:

> *Within Shiva there is Shakti, within Shakti there is Shiva. I see no difference between them; they are like the moon and the moonlight.*
>
> SIDDHASIDDHANTA SANGRAHA

It is also believed that through raising the *kundalini* power one is able to attain the *siddhis*.

All these things are bound-up with the idea of a subtle/psychic body that is mentioned in a variety of yogic and philosophical teachings in Hinduism, which is connected with the vital *pranic* life-force that permeates all things in the universe. *Prana* is comparable to *Chi* energy mentioned in Chinese traditions. Through practices, such as *pranayama*, students are able to become more aware of the *pranic* energy that works both within and around them, and open up to psychic and transforming spiritual realms of being and the powers that these can bring.

However, practices of *pranayama* are not undertaken in isolation from other exercises. The influential – in yogic circles – *Yoga Sutra* places such practices after the *yamas* (external ethical virtues) and *niyamas* (the cultivation of inner virtues), which include non-harmfulness, truthfulness and mindful introspection. As a whole, the *yamas* and *niyamas* are looked upon as indispensable practices in the various yogic traditions.

The powers in Buddhist spirituality

Many early Western interpreters of Buddhism saw the tradition essentially as a practical and an ethical path to spiritual freedom. Any mention of supernormal powers were either overlooked or explained away as later interpolations. However, the Buddha was well aware that the practice of meditation, which is seen as essential in his teachings for attaining enlightenment, led to the possession of the powers. The following is what the eminent Buddhist scholar Hellmuth Hecker pointed out about the powers in early Buddhist teachings:

> *The Pali suttas frequently ascribe supernormal powers to the Buddha and his arahant disciples, and there is little ground apart from personal prejudice for supporting*

39

such passages to interpolations.... when the suttas are considered in their totality, the clear conclusion emerges that the acquisition of paranormal powers was regarded as a positive good which serves to enhance the stature and completeness of the spiritually accomplished person.

Although it has to be said the Buddha believed that psychic or miraculous powers had limited value – the true aim being to transcend the world of unsatisfactoriness (*duhkha*) – and even goes as far to say he loathes the display of them in some of his teachings, such as the *Digha Nikaya* (1:213), there are accounts of him performing a whole series of them, which he does in order to help his disciples in some way, or to convert people (even though he would normally have converting people by preaching).

One of the Buddha's main disciples, Mahamggallana, was credited with various remarkable gifts, including clairvoyance, clairaudience and telekinesis. In one story about him (*Anguttara Nikaya* 7:58) he is described as suffering from fatigue and how, by using his psychic powers, the Buddha was able to suddenly appear before him and make his drowsiness disappear.

Another account about the Buddha (*Vinaya* 1:24-34), mentions how he asked three fire-worshipping brahmins if he could spend the night in a house where he is told there lives a supernatural cobra (*naga*) which might burn him up. (There have even been accounts of these supernatural cobras reported in modern times and of revered Buddhist holy men, such as Venerable Acariya Mun Bhuridatta

Thera, keeping them at bay.) The Buddha goes into the house and is unharmed, and after a while he is described as generating heat and flames which are seen in five colours. The Buddha then performs various other miracles, after which the brahmins are said to throw away their fire-worshipping equipment and convert.

Although an account such as this may well be meant to be interpreted allegorically to show the superiority of the Buddha and his path, and can also be seen as an example of him using 'skill in means' (a particularly essential practice in the Buddhist tradition), the important point is that the display or mention of miracles and supernatural powers is there in the early literature and is part of early Buddhism. What the Buddha normally objected to, was the unnecessary display of such powers. For instance, in the *Vinaya* (2:110-2), which holds teachings for the monastic community, the Buddha rebukes the *bikkhu*/monk Pindola for displaying supernatural powers merely to impress the laity.

As mentioned previously, Buddhism also teaches about six superknowledges, termed *abhinna* in the ancient Pali language, the language of the early Theravada Buddhist teachings. The first five can all be classed as ordinary miraculous powers that are found in various Indian traditions, and are bound-up with the Buddha's teachings on meditation and are identical with psychic powers found in Hinduism. It is believed that through various practices of meditation one can easily develop the five superknowledges of Buddhism, which include the divine eye, the divine ear, remembrance of past lives, reading the thoughts of others and numerous other gifts, such as seeing how the effects of previous karma influences people's rebirth. With the development of the divine ear, the *Visuddhimagga* (Theravada Buddhism's principal commentary on meditation practices) describes how one can hear the sounds of both human and divine beings from a great distance, as well as close-by.

Both the *Samannaphala Sutta* and the *Visuddhimagga* describe numerous others gifts (many of which are also found in Hindu spirituality), such as multiplying oneself many times, becoming invisible, walking through solid walls and mountains, diving in and out of the ground as though it were made of water, travelling through the sky (something the Buddha was said to have done), bilocation and producing a shower of water from the lower part of the body, along with fire from the upper part.

The five superknowledges themselves are considered as being fairly mundane in Buddhist teachings, and can be acquired by non-Buddhist masters of spirituality who have learned the art of meditation. Their display is not thought to imply that a true state of sanctity has been reached, but can indeed indicate that a certain level of progress has been achieved. It is the sixth superknowledge, which is about knowledge of how one overcomes all inhibiting traits – guaranteeing freedom from all restrictive worldly conditioning (*samsara*) – which is the most valued.

Although their description can be thought of as subjective states encountered while meditating, rather than physical demonstrations of miracles, the superknowledges are essential to the Buddha's teachings. In his experiences towards enlightenment, he personally opened up to many of them before touching a pure unconditioned state of awareness (Nirvana).

The powers are not actually looked upon as harmful in themselves, but as possible signs that an individual has suspended the laws of nature and overcome binding influences. But the Buddha warns us not to be tempted too much by them and so lose sight of the goal of liberation from birth, death and rebirth and other important areas of development, such as helping others – which he also classified as a type of supernormal power – to overcome their suffering.

An illustration of the Buddha's pragmatic approach to spirituality, is found in an account of him meeting an ascetic who told him that after 25 years, the path he was following had finally born fruit and was now able to cross the river he was sitting next to, by walking on the water. The Buddha was obviously unimpressed by the amount of time the man had wasted and pointed out that he could have just paid a ferryman one penny to take him across. Interestingly, to falsely claim possession of miraculous powers is one of four offences, which can lead to expulsion from the Buddhist monastic community, and ranks alongside killing, stealing and sexual misconduct. This in fact shows us how serious Buddhists monks are about the powers.

In Mahayana Buddhism, the Buddha himself is said

to have come back after his death (his *paranirvana*) and give further teachings at Vultures' Peak. A popular text/ teaching within the tradition, the *Abhidharmakosa* of Vasubanbhu (written around 5th century CE), gives an account of five powers which are attained in different ways: by meditation, by being inborn, by spells, by herbs, or by activities. In Tibetan Buddhism we find *The Tibetan Book of the Dead* mentioning that those who enter the *sidpa bardo* realm discover that they are endowed with the power of miraculous action (the ability to change shape, multiply oneself, become larger or smaller and disappear). This ability is described as arising naturally. However, the desire for it – according to Evans-Wentz in his translation of the book – Tibetan lamas say should be avoided until one is ready to use it and other psychic abilities wisely.

Milarepa, the great Tibetan yogi (1025-1135 CE), is reported to have possessed a number of psychic powers, including the ability to walk, rest and sleep while levitating. Various Tibetan ascetics are said to have produced spontaneous phenomena, such as leaving impressions in solid rock from where they have stood, sat or laid. In the meditation practice of *gTum-mo*, monks have been well documented in recent years to have generated heat in sub-zero temperatures, and within minutes, started to dry out dripping-wet, ice-cold blankets placed over them, which is done to test the proficiency of monks in the practice of *gTum-mo*.

The Vajrayana or Diamond Vehicle School of Buddhism – which is also referred to as Mantrayana because of the importance placed on mantra practices – is of particular significance. In this tradition the ability to employ a mantra properly, requires knowledge of using special psychic powers:

> ... *mantra gives power only to those who are conscious of its inner meaning, acquainted with its methods of operation and who know that it is a means to call up the dormant forces within us, through which we are capable of directing our destiny and of influencing our surroundings.*
>
> LAMA ANAGARIKA GOVINDA

In recent years we have seen the Sokka Gakkai branch of Buddhism claiming that by chanting before the ghonzon (a *mandala* inscribed with the words *namu myo-ho-renge-kyo*: 'hail to the wonderful truth of the Lotus Sutra'), has brought about such things as emotional and physical well-being, improved relationships with friends and family and, in some cases, has cured illnesses.

The Vajrayana tradition is acquainted with eight particular abilities, which represent various powers of mastery over the body, including such things as the elixir for the eyes that make the gods visible, the life-essence that preserves youth, fleetness in running, and the ability to fly and have control over spirits and demons. In the biographies of the eighty-four male and female *mahasiddhas* preserved in the Tibetan tradition, the attainment of these abilities is described in detail.

The actual title of *mahasiddha* roughly means 'a great

master of perfect abilities', and refers to a practitioner who has mastered the teachings of the *Tantras*. A yogi or yogini in any Indian tradition who attains enlightenment may be given the title of *siddha*. But the fact that this term is connected with the word *siddhi* indicates that it is primarily a form of spiritual awakening that connects strongly with psychic and miraculous abilities. Yet, as seen, within both Buddhist and Hindu spirituality, enlightenment is looked upon as something different to other powers and because of this it is sometimes described as the 'Supreme *Siddhi*'.

Prophets & Mystics

The powers in Jewish spirituality

One of the most fascinating things in the Jewish scriptures is the mention of angels. They are looked upon slightly differently, but no less significant, to how some might think of them today; for the Hebrew term *malakh*, meaning angel, is sometimes used in early sections of the Bible to refer to beings who have human form carrying God's message. In the account of the fall of Jericho, Joshia sees a man standing in front of him claiming he is a commander of the Lord (Josh. 5:13-14).

Only later did the term come to be used solely for spirit beings from heavenly realms acting as God's messengers. Gabriel and Michael are the only two angels mentioned by name in the Hebrew Bible. (Raphael and Uriel are mentioned in the books of the Apocrypha, a later collection of scriptures found in some Christian Bibles, which are not in the Jewish canon.) In the mystical teachings of the *Kabbalah*, an archangel is assigned to each emanation on the Tree of Life.

The influential Jewish philosopher, Maimonides (1135-1204 CE), believed that anyone entrusted with a mission was an angel – implying any person who had been touched by Divinity and had been inspired to help humanity in some way could be looked upon as having an angelic nature. Though modern Jewish spirituality does not deny the existence of angels, Biblical passages that refer to them are generally thought of as more symbolic and poetic.

One can see how the belief in angels continued in both the Christian and Islamic traditions. Similar to Spiritualists' beliefs, some Catholics believe in a personal guardian angel, though Spiritualists would usually prefer the term 'spirit guide'. The Islamic faith mentions four particular archangels – Izrail (the angel of death, who is not actually referred to by name in the Qur'an), Israfil (the angel who will announce the Day of Judgment), Gabriel (the angel who brings Divine revelation to people's hearts) and Michael (who holds important status with Gabriel) – along with the angels Munkar and Nakir (who question people on their first night in the grave about the Prophet Muhammad). In the Old Testament, Michael is the guardian angel of Israel.

Angels in the more traditional sense of the word are obviously seen as special beings and the ability to be aware of and be in contact with them could be considered as a form of clairvoyant, clairaudient or clairsentient ability. On the whole, the Bible looks upon the activity of angels as an assurance of God's involvement in the world. Their appearance often signifies God's presence. In fact some passages, where it refers to "the angel of the Lord", it is hard to know if it is the actual Presence of God or a separate agent being mentioned, as seen in Genesis, Chapter 16, Verses 9-13, where it uses the phrase and also mentions seeing God.

As well as angels, both the Old and New Testament make numerous references to the significance of dreams and their meanings and were also seen as important by the early Church fathers, including St. Augustine. Further to this, there are various famous nature miracles reported in the Book of Exodus, such as a strong wind causing the Red Sea to part (14:21). Elsewhere, there is mention of fire that is said to have fallen from the Lord to consume burnt offerings (1 Kgs. 18:37-38) and manna/food appearing at a time when the Israelites were wandering in the desert and in need of nourishment (Exod. 16:26-36). But it is difficult to say exactly how hungry the Israelites could have been, as they were only into the second month of their escape from Egypt and had taken dough for unleavened bread and large droves of livestock with them (Exod. 12: 34-38).

It has been speculated that manna may have been something that was secreted by insects or grew on tamarisk trees, which is known to have a sweet taste. But no matter how natural to the area it may have been, it was the way that it synchronisticly played its part in being there just when the Israelites were in need of food to sustain them that is looked upon as miraculous.

There are other miraculous happenings, such as accounts of healings mentioned in the Hebrew Scriptures, of which perhaps the most remarkable is recorded in the First Book of Kings (17:21-22):

> *He [Elijah] stretched himself upon the child three times, and cried unto the Lord, and said, O Lord my God, I pray thee, let this child's soul come unto him again. And the Lord heard the voice of Elijah; and the soul of the child came into him again, and he revived.*

Additionally, the Hebrew Bible contains numerous prophecies. A prophet, it ought to be said, is someone who is believed to have been appointed by God to spread God's message or teachings – sometimes reluctantly, as seen in the account of Moses and his ministry – or motivated by a higher justice to take action and protect the rights of those without a public voice. They are people who are often moved with the help of Divine inspiration to take compassionate action in times of great social injustice. Examples of such people in the 20th century are Mahatma Gandhi and Martin Luther King Jr., and more recently, the activist, physicist and ecologist Vandana Shiva has done much in the fight for justice in India.

The early prophecies of the Hebrews focus on revelations from God, which encourage the Israelites to find spiritual freedom, or on warnings for the Israelites to repent their sins and cease worshipping false gods and idols. But the idea of sin needs to be made clear here; for the Jewish faith holds no concept of original sin, which is a relatively late doctrine of the Christian Church that was not accepted until the 5th century CE, after being introduced by St. Augustine (354-430 CE). There is no fall of humankind that needs to redeem itself. Instead, one's original nature is seen as good, and life and Creation are viewed as Divine gifts from God. A young child's nature is held up as innocent and pure – a concept that is also held in Islam.

The central focus of the message or teachings of the prophets in the Hebrew Bible is generally concerned with encouraging individuals and/or the Israelites as a whole to keep to and follow a path of righteousness. The prophecies also tell of forthcoming events and give general warnings and comfort. Many of the first prophets prophesied in ecstatic states, in which it was believed the spirit of Yahweh/God possessed and spoke through them and through this they were able to guide the early Israelites.

Other Old Testament and Jewish Biblical prophecies mention the coming of the Messiah, who members of the faith believe will not come until the ruin of Solomon's Temple in Jerusalem is rebuilt.

At various times up to the present, some people have tried to relate Biblical prophecies concerning the future to their own times, with the belief that such things can never be wrong. Yet it has been shown that what such people are often doing is predicting after an event, which is technically known as 'retroactive clairvoyance'. Liberal thinkers of both the Jewish and Christian faith accept this view. Additionally, many passages of the Bible are open to all kinds of interpretation and one can arguably read just about anything into them if one puts one's mind to it.

In looking at the different areas of phenomena there can be a danger in focusing purely on them and overlooking the unshakable foundations of the Jewish faith, which are primarily concerned with the preservation of life (though a notion of 'stewardship' found in both Judaism and Christianity needs reassessing, as it implies that nature requires humans to have control over it, instead of learning how to live in harmony with it and find mutually beneficial enrichment), justice, the making of a better world and acting righteously and compassionately towards others, and what those with spiritual vision have to say to us today about their tradition's message.

Hillel, one of the most important figures in Jewish history, who lived in Jerusalem during the time of King Herod, was once asked to summarise the whole of the Torah while standing on one leg, to which he replied, "That which is hateful to you, do not do to others".

The highly influential contemporary Rabbi, Michael Lerner, encourages us to seek to connect our lives with the unfolding of the Spirit in the cosmos, with the creative healing and transforming energy of the universe, and to touch our authentic spiritual nature and realise it is a manifestation of the Ultimate Divine Presence in all. In his excellent book *Spirit Matters* he describes how the greatest joy in life comes from being able to recognise ourselves as part of the Unity of All Being and seeing that we are manifestations of love, goodness, joy and creativity.

For all life, he compassionately and movingly reminds us, is ultimately filled with Spirit.

The two interlocking triangles of the Jewish Star of David has been a popular symbol in many cultures since ancient times, which has been seen to represent the joining of two worlds, and of male and female energies coming together and the overcoming of opposites, thus representing harmony and unity and the integration of creative qualities.

The powers in Christian spirituality

Within the Christian tradition numerous miracles can be traced back to Jesus and the Old Testament. There is a tendency for some to think of Jesus as either a mystic or a medium with great healing abilities. But we must remember that for the majority of Christians, Jesus is neither of these, as he is looked upon – more through the eyes of John's Gospel, St. Paul and the resolution made by the First Council of Nicaea in 325 CE – as God, which some Hindus also believe, as they consider him to be an *avatar* (a Divine incarnation).

This belief may sit uncomfortably with some. But if we are to live harmoniously in a pluralistic society with people holding different beliefs, there needs to be an acceptance of difference, where we agree to disagree and respect others' paths to growth and seek out a common meeting ground where we can share the deeper mysteries and practices of a true spirituality.

Much is popularly known about the miracles of Jesus,

such as curing those who were blind, sick or lame, bringing Lazauras back to life, calming a storm, walking on water and turning water into wine. His miracles were seen by his followers to be signs that he was the expected Messiah and that God's new kingdom was about to come. However, for some Christians his miracles are not looked upon for authenticating his status, as he himself refused to perform them for that purpose (Matt. 12:38-39). But it is, perhaps, the way in which he is said to have both entered and left the world that are thought to be the most miraculous events in his life.

Jesus' virgin birth is told differently in two of the four canonical Gospels; it is also told differently in the Muslim Qur'an, which credits the infant Jesus with the ability to speak. It seems extraordinary that what is seen to be an important event in his life by many Christians is not mentioned in Mark's and John's Gospel (apart from an ambiguous passage in John 1:3 and a scant reference to Mary in Mark 6:3) and raises questions as to whether it was something that was added to the Gospels in an attempt to give more weight to Jesus' importance. Not all Christians believe in the virgin birth of course and accept that the retelling of a holy man's life can become more embellished and elaborated upon over the years. Many important figures in the past, such as Alexander the Great and the Buddha, were also credited with virgin births. Interestingly, the Gospel of Thomas and the contents of the speculated lost Q Gospel, focus more on Jesus' teachings rather than on his life and deeds.

The account of Jesus' resurrection is a different matter and is recorded in all of the four canonical Gospels, but each gives a different account of what actually happened. In Chapter 28 of Matthew's Gospel, it describes how Mary Magdalene and the "other Mary" find Jesus' tomb empty and how an angel tells them that Jesus has risen, after which they meet Jesus on their way to tell the disciples what had just happened. Or perhaps we should say 'other disciples', if we take the view of the Gospel of Mary Magdalene, which sees Mary Magdalene as one of the main disciples and fitting the role of an apostle herself.

The oldest of the canonical Gospels is Mark's Gospel, of which the original stops at Chapter 16, Verse 8 (Verses 9-20 were added later), and describes how Mary Magdalene and Mary, the mother of James and Salome, find the tomb empty and meet a young man in white who informs them that Jesus has risen.

In Chapter 24 of Luke's Gospel, Cleopas and another disciple are the first to be mentioned as seeing Jesus, and there are several women, including Mary Magdalene, who go to the tomb and find it empty, and are met there by two men wearing shining clothes, who ask them why they are, "looking for the living amongst the dead". In Chapter 20 of John's Gospel, only Mary Magdalene is said to have gone to the tomb and found it empty. After this she tells Simon Peter and the disciple Jesus loved, who then make their way to the tomb to see for themselves. It is only once they have gone home that Mary Magdalene then sees two angels in white, who ask her why she is crying and then sees Jesus, who tells her not to hold onto to him, as he has not yet returned to his Father.

The contradictions in the four Gospel accounts obviously makes one wonder just how much of them are reliable. But we have to remember that they are not historical documents, although some Christians try to use them this way, but are testaments of faith. In addition to this, the term 'resurrection' is symbolic language and can mean different things to different people. The finding of the empty tomb and Mary Magdalene's involvement as a chief witness are the only consistent elements. In analysis, the question has to be asked, as to whether an empty tomb implies that Jesus' physical body was actually resurrected or not. (Interestingly, there are stories of Tibetan yogis and lamas whose bodies are said to have disappeared on their death.) But the fact that women are featured so heavily in the Gospel accounts adds validity to them, as prejudice towards women in Jesus' time shows that they were not usually looked upon as reliable witnesses. Therefore, if someone was to fabricate a story of this kind during this period and wanted to convince others about its credibility, one would not have included women as central eye-witnesses, especially someone with Mary Magdalene's implied shadowy past.

We are never told exactly what it is she has done, but Luke's Gospel (8:2) tells us that seven demons were cast out of her. She is, however, one of Jesus' closest and most devoted followers. The idea of her being a prostitute is now accepted as a *later* interpretation of the Gospel texts, which was done deliberately to underplay the important role of women in the early Jesus movement. Many have considered Jesus as an early feminist because of his inclusive attitude towards women.

Jesus' famous saying, "I and the Father are One" (John 10:30), is his most fascinating statement. For some Christians it is thought to confirm his special Divine status (in Elaine Pagels' *Beyond Belief* she mentions that in the Jewish tradition in Biblical times, the titles 'son of God' and 'Messiah', which are connected to Jesus and have come to imply his Unique Divinity, would have designated someone who was Israel's human king). For others, the saying is seen as being no different to the insights of various mystics who realised in the deepest depth of their being there is a Supreme Sacred Oneness that connects us with all things. This corresponds more with the teachings of the Gospel of Thomas, which encourage us to realise that the kingdom of God is both within and all around us. Interestingly, some texts, such as the Gospel of Thomas, are sometimes referred to as 'apocryphal'. Although the word has come to imply an unreliable source of reference, it has its roots in the Greek language and actually means 'hidden' or 'secret' – implying that the teachings are meant to be understood more esoterically.

Jesus' transfiguration, where it is said his face shone like the sun and his clothes became as white as light (Matt. 17:2) or a flash of lightening (Luke 9:28), has become a popular episode in his life for some Spiritualists to identify with. There are indeed some parts of the event that are comparable to Spiritualistic types of physical phenomena, such as the materialisation of the deceased Moses and Elijah (Matt. 17:3 and Luke 9:30) and a discarnate voice that spoke to Peter, James and John (Matt. 17:5). The mention of the bright cloud that enveloped them (Matt. 17:2) was speculated by James F Malcolm to possibly be ectoplasm. But so little information is given about this cloud, we cannot really say what it was or why it is was there.

Another episode in the life of Jesus shows him having the ability to foretell his own death, which can be seen in Matthew's Gospel, where he tells his disciples that he will be handed over to be crucified (26:5). Controversially, the Gospel of Judas says Jesus planned his own death. John's Gospel describes his death as symbolically representing the Passover lamb. The idea held by many Christians about his death taking away the sins of the world, which draws on a passage in John's Gospel (1:29), has some similarities with a practice found in the Yoga tradition, where a guru may voluntarily take-on the karma of a disciple or community in order to advance their spiritual evolution.

In some ways I find it more fascinating to look at the lives of those who came after Jesus, as here we find people more like ourselves – instead of having the status of the saviour of all humanity attached to their importance – who are trying to make sense of the spiritual life and how to assess the use of various gifts that can unfold. Jesus, after all, said that those who believed in him would do even greater things than he did (John 14:12), so let us look at what some of these might be.

If we focus on the life of St. Paul we find that he is presented as a great miracle worker in the Acts of the Apostles and is credited with the power of healing. He is said to have performed exorcisms and cured a man who was sick with fever and dysentery, by laying his hands upon him.

St. Paul's letters to the Corinthians clearly show that various gifts were part of early Christian experience. He gave detailed instructions about the use of miracles, prophecy and healing (1 Cor. 12-14), as well as speaking in tongues, which first happened at the Feast of Pentecost after Jesus' death, where a sound like a violent wind came from heaven, and what is described as looking like tongues of fire rested on the apostles and other followers of Jesus and they began to speak in other languages (Acts 2:1-12) – an event that is often seen as the beginning of the Christian Church. However, St. Paul warns that if one has this gift or the ability to prophesies, or a faith that can move mountains, but does not have love, one has nothing (1 Cor. 13:1-3).

Later the practice of speaking in tongues was seen to be heretical by the established Church, but it has never died out completely. It was actually considered as a Divine gift by some saints who possessed or knew about others with the ability, whose very lives were seen to illustrate that it must have been given by God. However, today the Catholic Church in particular is generally suspicious of the ability to speak in a language of which one has no prior knowledge of.

If we look at the lives of some of the great Christian

mystics, we find various visions and other types of phenomena persistently appearing. St. Teresa of Avila (1515-1582) was said to have levitated several times and frequently had visions of angels. In one particular vision she experienced, which many academics have noticed has sexual overtones (which mystical experiences can have in relation to the idea of union), an angel manifested holding a spear of gold. At the tip of the spear there appeared to be a small fire. The angel then thrust the spear into her heart and then withdrew it. The experience left her feeling as though she was on fire and was immediately overwhelmed with a great feeling of love.

While praying on the mountain of Verna, St Francis of Assisi (1181-1226) is reported to have had a vision of a seraph (a six-winged angel) on a cross, which pierced him with the stigmata: the five wounds of Jesus. Other stigmatists, such as Padre Pio (1887-1968) and Therese Neumann (1898-1962), are reported to have had abilities of healing and bilocation, and to have performed various other miracles. Sometimes people witnessed a perfume emanating from Padre Pio, especially the odour of violets, lilies, roses and incense, even though as a Capuchin monk he would obviously not have worn perfume. The phenomena was seen as a sign that God had bestowed some grace on those who noticed it.

What comes over in the lives of the great mystics of the Catholic branch of Christian spirituality, is that they do not seek to attain supernatural gifts. Nor do they encourage others to possess them, as they are seen as a

Divine blessing, given by God. St. Teresa even advises beginners that it is best to resist them, believing the soul will advance quicker for doing so. The emphasis is on the practice of contemplation, prayer and spiritual conduct.

Nonetheless, although it appears that they do not seek the gifts, there are many accounts of them using them once they have manifested. St. Teresa's spiritual life and career as an abbess was governed by the voices she heard. The voices even warned her of coming events. Similarly, the medieval mystic Hildegarde of Bingen experienced various mystical visions throughout her life as an abbess, which guided her in the affairs of her convent. Similar to the accounts of Jesus, Padre Pio is said to have stroked the eyes of a young child and cured her blindness and to have helped a cripple to walk without the aid of crutches. On one occasion he told a woman he had dispelled the devil away from her.

But St. John of the Cross warned that the gifts can be used wrongly to deceive people and believed that there were some that were true and some that were not. Jesus also warned that, "Impostors will come claiming to be messiahs or prophets, and they will produce great signs and wonders to mislead ..." (Matt. 24:24).

On the whole, Catholic mystics appear unanimous in warning against attributing *too much* importance to the gifts. In chapter three of *The Ascent of Mount Carmel*, St. John wrote that joy in supernatural gifts and graces (what he termed the fifth class of goods) must be directed to God. He believed, as did St. Paul, that they are given for the benefit of others, and that joy in them

61

should be avoided. People, he felt, should rejoice not in the possession and exercise of the gifts themselves, but should seek and rejoice in the benefits of being able to serve God through them; for it is in charity, he believed, the fruit of eternal life lies.

This slightly negative view about possession of any gifts is given to encourage a sense of humility, though, as can be seen, the idea of having joy in them is not completely lacking. There is nothing wrong with humility of course, but I feel that there is equally nothing wrong with having a sense of awe and joyousness in the things that unfold on the spiritual journey. The contemporary writer on Creation Centred Spirituality, Matthew Fox, also encourages us to find a sense of awe and joy in the array of gifts we have, including those we may take for granted, such as the gift of parenthood, kindness and friendship.

On the subject of visions – whether objective or subjective – the Christian author Albert Farges pointed out the importance of examining them for clearness and detail: to distinguish between that which comes from nature, from God, from the imagination or the devil, although most Christians would not believe in the devil these days of course. If we put the latter into contemporary terms, we might think of the devil as a symbolic metaphor for the shadow part of our personality – that part of ourselves that stops us from growing, being inclusive in our evolvement, and realising our full creative and compassionate potential. Those who actually believe in a demonic realm invariably use it as a way of projecting the shadow part of themselves onto others, instead of owning it, and working with and transforming it and becoming more all-embracingly open to life.

Farges believed that genuine visions should appear spontaneously without preparation and disappear in the same manner. I can only assume he believed this as it would make less room for a vision to be coloured by our imagination. But, as we know only too well these days, the unconscious mind influences much of conscious experience, whether in a spontaneous mode or not.

Farges mentions two types of visions: clear and obscure. The obscure transcends ordinary imagery, which ties in with experiences found in other traditions, where the mystic is often lost for words to describe something beyond everyday realms of experience. The clear, reminds us how many mystical openings are intensely vivid and seem more dynamically real than regular perceptions. There is no loss of lucidity or vagueness about them when awakened to and experienced. Instead, they seem to bring about a wider understanding of the Reality and sacredness of all.

For many Christian mystics, the experience of clairvoyant visions and clairaudient voices are seen as a stage that may happen on the spiritual path. Interestingly, the Orthodox Church even uses the terms 'clairvoyant' and 'clairaudient'. But there are other stages, where what is sometimes called the 'mystic death' (seen sometimes as the death of the 'I' or ego, but a healthier view would be to consider it as a stage where the limitations of the individual 'I' are overcome, rather than a complete annihilation of it) or 'dark night of the soul' occurs, where the mystic is not always aware of any voice or visionary experience. In many ways Baptism can be seen as a ritual enactment of this stage on the mystical journey, where one dies, symbolically, and becomes a new person. It can seem like a spiritually dry period which is seldom lit by any uplifting experience, but it is usually looked upon as a stage of progression that can happen just before a profound awareness of a Supreme Unitive Consciousness is revealed, where the soul loses its separateness in the pure bliss and love of the Divine.

The renowned writer on Christian mysticism Evelyn Underhill believed that mystical visions and the hearing of mystical voices had a life enhancing quality about them, and were the means through which one truly approached God. In other words, that they are not only necessary phenomena for seeking union with the Divine, but are important experiences that bring about positive changes in an individual's spiritual growth:

> *They infuse something new in the way of strength, knowledge, direction; and leave it – physically, mentally, or spiritually – better than they found it.*
>
> EVELYN UNDERHILL

Similarly, Elaine Pagels, who has written much about Gnostic Christianity, points out that, "Without visions and revelations ... the Christian movement would not have begun". She even speculates whether,

Those who wrote, translated, and carefully copied works
such as the Secret Book of James and the Prayer of the
Apostle Paul may have known about techniques that
Jewish groups used to induce a state of ecstasy and invoke
visions.... Some of the Dead Sea Scrolls also offer prayers
and rituals apparently intended to help the devout enter
God's presence and join in worship with angels.

The powers in Islamic spirituality

The Qur'an, which literally means 'the recital', is held to
be the direct word of God by Muslims and is the most
sacred book of the Islamic faith. It is said to have been
revealed by the angel Gabriel to the Prophet Muhammad
while in various meditative trance-like states over a period
of approximately twenty years, until the latter part of his
life. The official Islamic accounts of Muhammad's life
(570-632 CE) say that he first encountered this experience
in the 7th century CE, when he was about forty years old,
while meditating in a cave in the outskirts of Makkah. The
Qur'an itself is looked upon by Muslims as a word for word
translation of a tablet that is eternally preserved in heaven.

The Qur'an does not use the word 'miracle', but
instead mentions the Arabic word *Ayat*, meaning 'signs'.
The Qur'an is in fact considered to have been created in
a miraculous way: as a Divine revelation. Because of this,
it is referred to and looked upon as a miracle itself. Some
Muslims have claimed that the Prophet Muhammad was
actually illiterate, and that this ads more weight to the
claim of their Holy Books being a miracle. Even if man

and *jinn*, a fiery spirit personality in Islam (it is believed that even people can sometimes turn into *jinns* when they die and can be of service to humankind), banded together to try to produce it, they would not be able to, the Qur'an tells us (17:90).

Although the Qur'an is seen as the principal miracle that happened in the life of the Prophet, the *Hadith*, which contains his sayings and numerous legends about him, attributes many other miracles to him, such as splitting the moon on one occasion when the people of Makkah requested to see a miracle. It seems like a particularly improbable claim if taken literally and was not reported to have been seen anywhere else in the world, which would be expected if such an event happened, though it has a certain amount of charm about it. But it is surprisingly similar to a passage found in Buddhist scripture about internal unity, which mentions how, "A monk who is skilled in concentration can cut the Himalayas in two" (*Anguttara Nikaya* 6:24).

There are accounts of the Prophet multiplying water and food on different occasions. Once there was not enough water for ritual washing before prayer time. Muhammad put his hand inside a vessel that contained only a small amount of water and then spread out his fingers. Water then gushed out like a fountain for everyone to use. There are other miracles and miraculous events that are said to have happened around Muhammad and performed by him, such as the restoring of a blind man's sight, and rocks and mountains being heard to speak and pay tribute to him.

But it is perhaps the Prophet's miraculous night journey (the *miraj*) that is the most fascinating. *Sura/* Chapter 17 in the Qur'an mentions how he was transported from the town of Makkah to Jerusalem, where he then ascended to heaven, accompanied by the angel Gabriel. There he conversed with Moses and was given the obligatory prayers for the followers of the faith. Afterwards, he was taken back to Makkah. The famous Dome of the Rock in Jerusalem is said to mark the exact spot where he ascended to heaven.

Scholars and Muslims alike have adopted different standpoints about this significant event. Some have interpreted it as a dream that the Prophet had, while others believe it was actually his physical body, or at the very least his spirit body, that was transported to both Jerusalem and heaven.

In considering the overall teachings of the Qur'an, we ought to remember that they are not trying to promote a new religion, but are looked upon by Muslims as a continuation of the older Judaeo-Christian tradition. The teachings accept the Torah, the Gospels, the early Jewish prophets and Jesus as early revelation, although they attempt to undermine further prophetic insights by claiming Muhammad to be 'the Seal of the Prophets' (33:40) – the last in the line of prophets linking with the Bible. But some Islamic scholars, such as Wilfred Madelung, have thought that the meaning of the term is not so certain.

Interestingly, even within the Islamic tradition, there has been some careful wordplay used to subtly attempt to steer around the statement and what it is thought to imply, which can be seen in an idea about 'the Seal of the Saints', put forward by Ibn 'Arabi (1165-1240 CE) – one of Sufism's (the main mystical branch of Islam) greatest teachers – in which he sees himself as being the last to receive esoteric teachings because of his spirit being identical with Muhammad's. But this idea actually contradicts 'Arabi's own teachings about 'One Essence', in which everyone's spirit is seen as identical and, therefore, there should be no reason why 'Arabi's spirit is more special than or favoured over anyone else's.

Another important Sufi was Hallaj, who was executed in Baghdad in 922 CE. He was associated with numerous miraculous abilities. He studied with the renowned Sufi Junayd in Iraq, but broke away after a quarrel about following the path of the heart (called the 'drunken school' in Sufism) rather than the head (the 'sober school' in Sufism), and later became a popular figure in Iran. He personally preferred to follow the path of devotion to God. He stopped wearing the woollen garment of the early Sufis and began to preach in public, as well as travel to places such as India and Central Asia.

He was eventually accused of performing magic and miracles and was arrested and thrown into prison. Some, it is said, accused him of blasphemy, and others, of being a secret Christian. Some lesser-minded Sufis accused him of believing that both human and Divine nature could be harmonised. In addition to this, others felt that an idea he held about incarnation was not acceptable, as it implied having two separate essences that could be united; for if you are already God in essence, which some of his sayings appear to have suggested, then you cannot 'become' what you already are!

The main reason for his execution, it seems, was more to do with his teaching that the pilgrimage to Makkah could be done in one's own home, and shows a lack of tolerance for diverse views and free-thinking starting to enter the Islamic faith. His execution sent shock-waves through the Sufi tradition and put many of them on their guard.

The miracles, according to reports, were genuine and ranged from apporting fruit, to making his whole body fill an entire room. Similar to Jesus, a popular saying of his was, "I am the Truth, I am the Real", which is a famous saying in Islam – the Divine is often referred to as 'the Real' in Sufism.

In many ways Hallaj exemplified the deepest possibilities of personal piety to be found in Islam. He demonstrated the true meaning of submission to the unity of the Divine Beloved – not with the aim of gaining any form of personal sanctity, but in order to live and teach the deeper mysteries of a devotional life.

In the biographies of Islamic saints and mystics, there are accounts of both men and women who penetrated Divine Truths through their devotion to a spiritual way of life and living. The many miracles that have been credited to them is part of mainstream Islamic belief. The *Aqida Tahawi*, which is a summary of Sunni beliefs, mentions the marvels of the saints and affirms the stories about them. Similar to the powers of Jesus and various yogis, their saints are credited with being able to fly, walk on water, foretell the future and travel hundreds of miles in one step.

In modern times we could draw upon one of the world's leading exponents of Islamic science and spirituality, Seyyed Hossein Nasr, who points out that Oneness is the highest of all experience and gifts, and how in its ultimate sense this belongs only to God as the Absolute, which he universally describes as 'Brahman, Allah, the Godhead, and the Highest and Ultimate Reality'. His writings on Sufism have a contemporary feel about them, are all-embracing, and focus on a profound spirituality, which is about how it is only the Spirit that is able to bring about an integration and unity of the psyche, intellect and mind. This implies both a vertical transcendence in order to discover the Divine, and an embodiment of Divinity which horizontally embraces It in our lives and exhibits natural act of compassion as a result of this discovery:

> *The supreme formula for unity in Islam is that 'There is no Divinity but God'. That the Divine is all, in all and transcends all. The ultimate practice for Sufi's is not to pray at all times, but for one's life to become a constant act of prayer. For God is always present in all things.*
>
> SEYYED HOSSEIN NASR

Bringing the Strands Together

It can be seen that each tradition takes a slightly different stand about miraculous powers and how they manifest, and that even within each tradition there are diverse views. On the one hand, Roman Catholic mystics do not aim to attain the gifts; for if they are *gifts from God* and seen as a sign of Divine grace, then they can only be acquired as a gift, rather than by personally developing them. On the other hand, St. Paul advocated the desire for spiritual gifts, especially prophecy (1 Cor. 14:1).

The superknowledges in Buddhism, as well as the *siddhis* in the *Yoga Sutra*, are, nonetheless, attained through one's own efforts, and are basically aimed for in order to help overcome the effects of karma and achieve liberation, though some of the powers appear to be more by-products of certain practices in the *Yoga Sutra*.

According to Swami Prabhavananda and Christopher Isherwood, Aphorism 321 of the *Yoga Sutra*, recommends giving up the powers if one wishes to attain liberation from the ties that bind us. This is a popular view which some hold – that only by renouncing the powers is a yoga practitioner able to achieve the higher spiritual goal – and has arisen through a belief in the world being an illusion (*maya*) by some non-dualistic teachers of Hindu philosophy and, therefore, anything belonging to the world, including psychic powers, has little value. This is in fact a misleading interpretation of the *Yoga Sutra* and has created some uninformed prejudice in some circles. The idea of seeing everything as an illusion is also a dangerous belief if taken to the extremes of seeing nothing as valid or real in life, as it can lead to a lack of care for the Earth and others.

Although mystics and contemporary scientists both tell us that life is not as it appears, i.e. as being made up of individual separate phenomena, it does not imply that everyday experience does not have a level of reality and should not be a part of the spiritual life. The great Vedantist philosopher Shankara (788-820 CE), who influenced many ideas about life as an illusion in Hinduism, drew upon the analogy of seeing a rope as a snake. If one thinks about this analogy, one can see that it is more about misperceptions and not seeing things as they really are, which does not imply that nothing is real and everything is an illusion.

In contrast to Prabhavananda's and Isherwood's comment about the powers, the translation by J. H. Woods, describes the same passage of the *Yoga Sutra* as being about 'having no cause for attachment or pride'. The excellent and always practical yoga writer and practitioner Georg Feuerstein points out in his version of the *Sutra* that, "The popular opinion that these yogic abilities are not part of the path to Self-realisation is demonstrably wrong.... they *cannot* be separated from the essentially organic and

72

unitary structure of Yoga".

Elsewhere in the Hindu spiritual tradition, although popular devotional texts, such as the *Bhagavata Purana*, tell us that the gifts are 'given by God' – instead of being developed through practices – they can be seen to be partly earned through one's own efforts, as the devotee has to deliberately meditate on a feature of God to have them bestowed upon him or her. However, it should be mentioned that the powers are not primarily sought after or given for the attainment of mastery over the elements, but for mastery over one's self. This view seems to apply to the whole yogic tradition. For it is the attainment of spiritual freedom, and not the actual powers themselves, which indicates true progress.

According to the religious studies scholar Mircea Eliade, "he who succumbs to the desire to use them ultimately remains a mere 'magician,' without power to surpass himself". But contrary to this, it can be seen that having been attained, the powers are often used in different spiritual traditions. Christian mystics believe they can be used as a way of service to God. Ancient brahmin priests used their powers in the belief that they were helping to maintain cosmic order. The Buddha used them for the purpose of conversion and on the nights of his enlightenment. Even today, Buddhists and Hindus sometimes seek help from a teacher whose compassion for humanity, in conjunction with his or her special gifts, might be called upon to benefit others in their community, and the belief in the power of prayer is held by millions of people throughout the world.

Why some yogis, such as Gopi Krishna, advocated not using the gifts, especially as it can be seen that some of them are used in order to become aware of unconscious influences (*samskara*) and help undo the effects of binding karma, may well be because they wanted to focus people's attention more on the spiritual dimensions of their tradition, rather than on the sensational.

I do not see reasons why those naturally endowed with gifts of healing, for example, should need to deny or suppress them, as not only would it create a psychological imbalance, but it would also stop them from co-operating with the Creative Divine Mind of the universe. Would it not be better to use all gifts we have selflessly and wisely, and allow them to lead us to a wider understanding of spirituality?

Where all traditions appear to agree, is in warning that miraculous powers should not be sought after for their own sake, or be used to reinforce one's self-importance. The emphasis for taking a spiritual perspective is generally on humility, non-attachment, living virtuously and other practices, such as the cultivation of insight, mindfulness and compassionate actions.

It ought to be said that to be classed as a mystic – or even as a spiritually aware person – one need not display or possess any miraculous powers at all, other than the above things mentioned, although technically a true mystic is someone who is seeking to bring his or her life in harmony with God in some way. In Islam, miracles are not necessarily looked upon as a condition of sainthood, although they are often found in abundance in the biographies of their saints. On the whole, Muslim teachings encourage us to look for signs of righteousness, which signify that one is on the right track for living a truly spiritual life.

As pointed out in this book, Buddhists generally agree that the display of any miraculous power – other than the sixth superknowledge, which overcomes all inhibiting patterns – does not always indicate that someone has reached a genuine stage of growth. In his *Autobiography of a Yogi*, Paramahansa Yogananda also stated that, "Spiritual advancement is not to be measured by one's display of outward powers ...". However, we need to be clear here and mention that Yogananda is not referring to powers of compassion or other comparative exterior acts of spirituality, but to the exhibition of traditionally understood psychic and miraculous powers and abilities.

In a documentary series made for English television (called *Transformations*), the English Benedictine, Father Bede Griffiths, mentioned how Roman Catholicism had mistakenly viewed supernormal powers as being either from God or from the devil, whereas in India the distinction between the psychic and the spiritual had been more accurately understood. "In India", he pointed out, "they have recognised that there is a vast psychic realm, which is neither good nor bad; it is ambivalent".

I think it is essential to bear Father Bede's observations in mind and to realise that it is how the gifts or powers are used and influence our life and conduct that truly determine their worth.

The ultimate gifts and wisdom of wholeness and unity

In looking at teachings about psychic, mediumistic and miraculous powers, there is a danger in searching for the purely historical over the ever-present universal Divine Consciousness – the God in all that is eternally creating within our cosmos. The French priest, mystic and paleontologist Teilhard de Chardin, who was one of the most forward looking Christians of the last century, was not so concerned with the historical Jesus, but in relating to the presence of the evolving Cosmic Christ/immanent God Consciousness, which unites all species and permeates all.

The great seers, mystics and prophets of the past described the powers through the eyes, terminology and understanding of their time. Yet some wisdom and insights of our current age may require us to let a few perspectives and ancient beliefs go, or at least to reassess them. Some of the miracles of Jesus, for example, where he is reported to have cast out demons, look as though he was in fact helping people suffering from epileptic seizures (Matt. 17:14-15) or psychological disturbances (Matt. 8:28-34).

We know now that many experiences are conditioned by our held beliefs and concepts, which can be reinforced by the views of others that we share our beliefs with. Nonetheless, this does not imply that the experiences that unfold on the road to spirituality will have no value, or life enhancing qualities about them, but merely that they can often draw upon the symbols and beliefs that have some meaning for us, of which we can identify with.

The search is always ongoing and calls us to look freshly for answers from the understanding of our current age and invariably requires us to step out of our current thinking in order to discover a greater perspective. We know only too well that traditions can become institutionalised and unhealthily concerned with trying to get everyone to sign-up for a set creed or doctrine. But generally, this is not how they started. With the discovery of the Gnostic Gospels and other texts at Nag Hammadi in 1945, we have come to see how the early Christians were similar to some modern seekers and held many beliefs, and how spirituality was for them more about a continual and personal quest for Truth and transforming oneself.

Yet we will never be in a position where we have all the answers of course; for that would not only take away the mystics' – of which we all are, as ultimately we each share a sense of oneness and unity with the Divine – profound sense of awe and wonder, but would also bring our evolvement to a complete and uncreative standstill.

I think Bede Griffiths' following observation is also worth considering when it comes to the psychic realm, as the point he makes is noticeable at times and it reminds us that because of the nature of experiences discovered within it, that it is a world where oneness and unitive states of consciousness and the transforming awareness that these can bring, are not always present:

As long as we are in the psychic world it is a world of

multiplicity. There are many gods, many angels, many spirits, many powers of various sorts and this is why the psychic world is always somewhat ambiguous.

What comes over clearest and as the most important in the lives and teachings of various mystics, Buddhas and yogis is the quest for spirituality (instead of religious barriers) – compassion and loving one's neighbour being the greatest gifts, and discovering a peace, wisdom and an equanimity that helps us to put our finer qualities to use in practical ways. The parable of the good Samaritan demonstrates how compassionate actions are more important than beliefs and rituals and is something we should not forget.

Buddhists place much emphasis on daily life practices. Within Hinduism there is karma yoga, which is about making all of our actions skilful and mindful and is perhaps comparable in some ways to the practice of mindfulness in Buddhism. In Islam and Christianity there has often been work done for the poor and sick (charity being one of the Five Pillars of Islam).

For the powers themselves, when used by those who have not reflected upon the broader implications of spirituality, can even divide its followers into those who are seen to have the gifts and those who have not, whereas in reality everyone is endowed with worthy abilities, but it is how we use them that makes them spiritual and profoundly effective. A healthy spirituality values *all* creative abilities and areas of development and helps them to flourish; for our authentic nature is the key to infinite creative potential, which is available for us to use in every moment.

What contemporary science, such as Quantum physics and Rupert Sheldrake's theories about morphogenetic fields, is confirming is the insights of some of the great mystics and early indigenous beliefs into the non-separate interrelatedness of nature and all existence. Such knowledge needs to move us to consider how numerous holistic, integral and spiritual practices can help us to touch life more deeply and bring about mutually beneficial enrichment to the needs of all.

If the whole is not included in development it can cause a split between the individual and other spheres of life – the Spirit world and the physical world are not two separate things – and leave the door open to an unnatural balance of power where those with certain gifts have the final say and cannot be questioned, which disencourages free thinking, a spiritually mature acceptance of difference and the wisdom which is within everyone to be truly appreciated and helped to grow.

It is not that the Spirit, the Divine and the realms of spirituality are in the possession of only a certain few, as is often seen in unhealthy cults and fundamentalist strands of belief. The Ultimate Reality is that *everyone* is in touch with these in an infinite variety of different ways. They are bound-up with and work through all, including ourselves and the Earth we walk on. We are, after all, a part of and connected to the Earth and nature. A true guru/teacher in Hinduism will help students to discover the Ultimate Guru, which is universal. For the Hindu philosopher

79

Ramanuja (11th century CE), the whole world was seen as Vishnu's/God's body.

The roads that lead to spirituality are eternally calling us; all we have to do is be responsive and willing to evolve with the spiritual universe in which we live, of which all life is a unique expression. A deep sense of unity with this One in all and all in One can lead us to profound awakenings that exist in every moment and to wholesome actions that healthily participate in life as it unfolds.

Realms of spiritual being

We often see various gifts coming to the fore quite naturally when students develop the many facets of their spiritual nature – an approach that can supply them with the knowledge of how to handle their gifts wisely. To develop any ability without a spiritual basis for good is to be drawn away from the whole of our creative potential and the richer possibilities that can be available to us.

The most important openings lead us to skilfully acts of compassion, to wisely and deeply connecting with the unfolding mysteries of life and the universe, to caring for the Earth and all its inhabitants and biological diversity. For within us there is the Creative Divine Impulse, which is full of wondrous gifts of numerous kinds; not just psychic, shamanistic or mediumistic ones, or the traditionally considered miraculous. For just being is miraculous. Rabbi Abraham Heschel reminds us that, "Just to be is a blessing. Just to live is holy". But how often are we aware of this miraculousness, this blessing and holiness? How often do we take part in and celebrate the creativity that flows through all and co-operate in the unfolding of it in life?

When there is an awakening to the spiritual realms of being, it is only natural that every moment and facet of our lives will start to become more harmonious and begin to reach out to deeply embrace and include all (other life, people, faiths and the Earth) in a unifying whole.

We have to remember why the Buddha, Muhammad, the Jewish prophets, Jesus and many of the great yogis and yoginis are remembered. The Buddha in particular, is primarily respected throughout the world for his insights into the human condition, his teachings on non-violence, loving-kindness, transforming all that inhibits our true nature and how to live in harmony with life and find peace in every step.

Without a holistic message of a compassionate unity that transcended religious dogmas and social divisions, Jesus would have soon been forgotten. Muhammad's wisdom, and his everyday life and conduct, are held up as examples for Muslims to live by, and the central message of the Qur'an is one of peace and surrender to the *spiritual will* of the Divine – a life of non-harm and brotherhood and sisterhood with others ("Let there be no compulsion in religion" the Qur'an states: 2:256). For the majority of Muslims, the true message of Islam is about equality, an acceptance of differences, and to be a patient, respectful and loving person, with no discrimination or unwholesome qualities.

A popular prayer from Jewish scripture calls upon God to establish peace, goodness, blessing, graciousness, kindness and compassion upon us all and upon the people of Israel. The prophetic message of Micah in the Hebrew Bible, reminds us that every individual has an obligation to both God and his or her community to act justly, be merciful and walk humbly with God (6:8).

Throughout human history, every age has seen those who have distorted such teachings and spiritual examples of being human in order to exclude others for political ends and for self-gain, or because of a lack of understanding. But the real heroes are those who have lived by teachings of harmony, inclusiveness and unity in diversity, who were invariably inspired at certain times in their lives to call for compassionate action and to speak out when human rights were threatened. In today's world we also have to consider the rights of non-human species and include the preservation of nature, of which we are intrinsically bound-up with.

On the matter of spiritual inclusiveness I would like the last words to go to the always inspirational and ecumenical teacher and activist Matthew Fox, from his recent book *The A.W.E. Project, Reinventing Eduction, Reinventing the Human*:

> *From Buddha to Jesus, from Isiah to Muhammad, from Black Elk to the Vedas of India, from Lao Tzu to the wisdom teachers of Africa, our species is admonished to respond to life with Compassion. Gandhi and Martin Luther King, Jr. are just two who have become 20th century heroes for having done so.*

Appendix 1
A Conversation with Glyn Edwards on the Powers

Glyn Edwards, who is also known by the yoga/spiritual name Devadasa (servant of God), is internationally recognised as one of the UK's finest mediums and intuitives. He joined a Benedictine community at sixteen, which intensified his mediumistic awareness and eventually led him back into the world. Since then he has travelled extensively, speaking, lecturing, demonstrating and running workshops worldwide, and helped to found the Gordon Higginson Fellowship for Integral Spirituality. He has been a regular senior course tutor at the Arthur Findlay College (a college for the study and advancement of psychic science) for over three decades. He has also worked at the Spiritualist Association of Great Britain and has been involved with the research of PRISM (Psychical Research Involving Selected Mediums).

The following conversations with Glyn took place in London and were especially arranged for them to be included in this book. Interestingly, although he had read an early draft of the book, in some places he raised points about spirituality and development that were similar to ones that I was working on for extra passages, which seemed to show some synchronistic thinking happening between the two of us. In other places he brought in other perspectives that drew deeply on his beliefs and experience as a medium. Questions put to him were invariably followed by a period of reflective silence. He would then answer fluently without pausing until he had covered all that he felt was needed to be said.

*   *   *

S: When did you start to notice that you had the abilities you have? Have they caused you any problems in your development and what has been the spiritual implications of these abilities?

GE: I can remember having experiences that could be classed as mediumistic when I was around four years old. But it was not until I was older and at about the age of eighteen that I realised the significance of these experiences. In my teenage years I experienced what could be classed as a spiritual crisis, as the experiences were making me take a much broader view of some of the things I had been brought up to believe, and when I started to investigate and be involved in Spiritualistic fields of work I also encountered problems, but of a different kind. As certain abilities unfolded, I was given advice that now seems to me to be limiting and does not take into account the spiritual whole of our being. For instance, I was often given the impression that gifts such as mediumship, healing and teaching were abilities that worked separately from one another and if I concentrated on only one area it would not necessarily help with the development of other abilities. But as I progressed I found that this was not the case. Like a layer upon layer, I discovered that all abilities are interconnected, as they are after all part of one's being and link us with the creativity of all life. It is through this that I discovered the need to be open to and realise the oneness and wholeness of spiritual development.

I realised that any kind of healthy development needed to include and work with many facets of our being – including conflicting parts or any set-backs on the spiritual path – in order to unfold an integrative awareness of a sacred wholeness, which has the power to bring balance in our lives, and from which we realise the True Centre of our being that radiates out through all that we are and do. I realised that there could be no limits or boundaries placed on the Ultimate Essence of our being; for if the Divine is limitless and in all, and all is in the Divine, then the creative abilities we have must also be limitless.

I have come to see that the spiritual potential within us is not confined; it is we who place restrictions on it. In my early years I realised that I had to be careful when listening to those who sought to impose rigid beliefs about a separation between different areas of life. What I have now found is that we need to find a sense of freedom within ourselves to face the journey of unfoldment, from which comes a discovery of an inclusive and compassionate understanding that trusts and nurtures the whole of our being. Ultimately, the spirit, the True Self that we are, is deathless, changeless and full of infinite positive potential and seeks harmonious expression through all.

S: The spirit world as mediums and shamans generally think of it is not always there in the same way in other traditions. Can you possibly explain why? Further to this, mediums and shamans often paint a physical and dualistic view of the after-life that seems rather like life as we already know it, except with a spirit body instead of a physical one. Contemporary science, as well as many mystical insights, talk more about an interconnected Oneness. Where do you stand on this?

GE: An interconnected Oneness fits more with my own understanding. Beliefs, as we know, are invariably influenced by the cultures we grow up in and even spiritual experiences are influenced by set beliefs. It is easier for us to grasp aspects of a spiritual dimension if we think of it in similar ways to everyday life. For some, it is a helpful way of relating to the spirit world. But one can see that it creates a sense of physicality about it, as a means to explain a dimension that is ultimately bound-up with and interacting in and through all.

All the great wisdom traditions have beliefs about an after-life, yet all have slightly different perspectives. When it comes to beliefs, I feel we have to consider the point you raised in this new book and fleshed out in *The House of Wisdom*, about 'I am right and you are wrong' approaches, as they can only lead to divisions and conflicts, instead of a respectful acceptance of difference, or a mature spirituality which allows us to agree to disagree, without being unsettled by another person's opinion.

For me and knowledgeable teachers I have felt privileged to have met from numerous disciplines – and if one looks at what some of the great spiritual teachers of history have had to say about what this other dimension encompasses – there are realms where we go beyond concepts and definitions.

I believe, just as physical existence is, that the life of a disembodied spirit personality is evolving toward an interrelated state of pure being and consciousness, that is about unity and interconnectedness, rather than individual separateness. As to how much my own acquired beliefs have influenced this view, who can say. However, contemporary scientific investigations are starting to confirm much of this understanding, which can be traced back to the insights of various mystical traditions. I do feel, however, that prevalent beliefs we hold prior to and after-death of the physical body, can create the image of a physical realm. But from my experience as a medium, this image appears to be quickly dropped as a wider expanse of experience is awakened to.

Other areas of interest are found in the way some spirit communicators describe after-death states as being similar to our physical world and yet others do not. We will have to decide for ourselves what is true or not, instead of relying on what others tell us to believe.

An individual may undergo spiritual and mediumistic types of experience that seem very real to him or her. However, modern psychology warns us that all experiences are invariably coloured by present, as well as past, systems of belief and previous experience. I think we have to be careful about seeing things as either black or white and accept that there are many grey areas of development, before arriving at a clear understanding about some things. This after all is what the word 'development' implies – an ongoing process of evolvement, which includes an evolvement of our beliefs.

Discovering spiritual truths does not always happen over night. We need to encourage each other and ourselves to work deeply and probe within ourselves and any experiences or openings we have in order to arrive at what is truly valid and ultimately real. For me, one test for contemplating whether something is spiritually valuable or not, is if it allows for an inclusion, acceptance and compassionate embracing of others. If it does not, it surely has not gone far enough; for it has not reached that understanding of an interconnected Oneness that you mentioned.

S: What is your view on grace? Are the powers already there – inherent in everyone – given as a Divine blessing as a form of grace, or are they developed?.

GE: This is a good and important question. However, here we are again entering into the realms of belief and it also depends on one's definition of grace. For me, grace is a sense of giving and receiving, which happens not just between the Divine and Its creation, but is also transmitted from our own human self to others. Ultimate realms of development transcend terms and concepts, yet at the same time we need them to individually understand certain things about spiritual growth and development. Grace is a mystical element of growth that is difficult to pin-down to being just one thing. You were telling me recently how in the Jewish faith, life and Creation and its abundance and beauty are seen collectively as a form of God's grace, which is quite a valid view I think.

Grace has within it elements of love, compassion, understanding, wisdom and kindness. It is something that enlarges the mind, our processes of thought, perception and awareness, and all actions and activities of life. It affects every level of who and what we are, and helps us to unfold altruistic and Divine qualities in our lives. It can, therefore, be seen as an important and essential facet of unfoldment, which is sometimes overlooked or not mentioned enough in some spiritual teachings.

As to whether psychic, mediumistic or miraculous gifts or abilities are given or developed is something I can only answer from my own understanding. As far as I can see we are born with a predisposition for these abilities. From my experience, these abilities take us into the realms of potential and, therefore, into areas of individual possibilities. It is through recognition, receptivity, opening our minds and working with our potential that an awareness of there being no limit to the abilities that we have comes into being. It is we who place limits and conditions on them. From the supreme perspective it can be seen as the Divine within us awakening and opening to Itself so, therefore, why would It hold anything back from Itself?

Psychic, mediumistic and miraculous powers in this sense are neither given or developed, but are 'revealed' when we remove all that stops us from recognising them as an inherent part of our nature. Development in this area then lies more in how we reach this level of understanding and manifest such powers more purely. For those who wish to explore more about this profound view of spiritual unfoldment, the books by the Christian writer Joel S. Goldsmith are particularly strong on this point of understanding about grace and how God, the Divine, is the Ultimate Power in our unfoldment and in the universe.

S: In mediumistic trance-states, there appears to be a loss of consciousness and lucidity. Some reputable mediumistic writers, such as Lawrence and Phoebe Bendit, whose books are published by the Theosophical Society, feel that it is not a healthy thing to develop because of this. It also seems to go against mystical traditions' ideas, especially yoga and Buddhism, about a clarity of mind. What are your views?

GE: Here we are entering into an arena which is difficult to fall on any one side. If you look at the teachings of the past and present about trance-states and how they can affect a medium, there are various views about them.

Some mediums describe a loss of awareness and lucidity experienced in some trance-states as actually enhancing their conscious life, because another mind separate from them has awakened them to something greater than they had originally realised. After being in a mediumistic state of trance, and once the medium has come back to full consciousness and lucidity, the impression left behind in his or her unconscious mind (I use the word 'unconscious' here, because in a way he or she has been unconscious to normal surroundings) is described by some to have benefited their life. Some are said to feel healthier, happier and to have a much more expanded view of life, because they have opened to another spiritual mind that has blended with them. However, there are others I have known who have talked of a reverse effect.

In certain areas of spirituality, mystics in different wisdom traditions describe entering into states of ecstatic awareness in which their consciousness of physical life ceases to exist. Yet areas of psychological research tell us that some yogis and yoginis who enter into various advanced states of *samadhi*, actually experience heightened beta brain-wave activities, which are more typically found in intense concentration or even in periods of agitation. Yogis and yoginis themselves tell us that what they experience is more of an awakened state, rather than a loss of consciousness. I think more investigation needs to be done in this area to define what appears to be different types of experience and how they can affect people in different ways. But it seems to me that many mystics are experiencing what can be described as trance-like ecstatic states of awareness.

In the psychology of yoga and Buddhism, although they both emphasise a clarity of mind, they also promote meditative practices that are bound-up with altered-states of awareness, which can be viewed as forms of entrancement. The practice of *pratyahara* in yoga, for example, is about the withdrawal of the senses from outward distractions and can be seen as a kind of preliminary trance-like state of awareness.

On returning to everyday awareness, mystics from various traditions sometimes described the deep experiences they have as leaving them feeling exhausted, debilitated or challenged in some way. Yet they also describe, as mediums have, that it heals them, enhances their being and awareness and deepens their spirituality. Some mystics have described how their experiences created an inner conflict between their spiritual and worldly selves. This is an area were modern therapeutic approaches to spiritual development can help in bringing about a balance and a harmony between the appearance of different and sometimes opposing parts of our nature, and reveal a more congruent and truthful life.

There are mediums that tell us that the trance-states they have undergone, with a loss of conscious awareness, has unfolded what they describe as a clarity of mind that is 'perhaps' comparable to what some yogis and Buddhists describe. It is difficult to say one thing or the other. We need to look more closely at what these various states can bring about within the individual, without imposing beliefs, but decide for ourselves whether the unfoldment of these states is desirable or not for one's overall well-being and growth.

We need to be careful before deciding what is useful or not in development, as there are clearly realms within realms of awareness where it is hard to draw a clear line and say that this is right and something else is wrong. We must search as widely as we can and decide what is beneficial and right for our growth. There is much food for thought in the Bendit books – and all views can help us to arrive at a spirituality that is more thought-through and life enhancing – but we need to remember that everyone is teaching from their own experience and perspectives and that others may see things differently.

In the mediumistic trance-state there have been those who have entered into it and given evidence of survival after-death and various spiritual teachings, yet these have had no effect upon the medium's behaviour, or changed them for either good or bad. This seems to show that this other world is not here to impose its will upon us, but leaves us to decide for ourselves whether to inculcate the teachings and the implications of an eternal spiritual life.

There have been mystics, such as Rasputin, that evidently had remarkable powers, and were able to enter into trance-like states, which did not outwardly improve them in any way. I think it is extremely important that we keep an open mind, that we are objective and non-judgemental where trance-states are concerned, as it is a wide topic and there are many facets to consider.

S: *Is there a danger in feeling important and somehow separate from others because of the gifts?*

GE: Yes, of course. We have to be realistic and remember that these abilities do not set us apart from everyday life. If approached from a spiritual perspective, they can enable us to engage more healthily with life as it unfolds, rather than standing apart from it.

These gifts or abilities, whatever one wishes to call them, can lead us to sharing in others' joys and suffering, instead of thinking that we are in some way more important than other people.

If we consider some of the excellent work that has been done by some medical doctors, the selfless actions of many nurses throughout history, the kindness of those who have helped build a better world in which to live, the insights into the heart of spiritual development some have had (which have become major influences for humanity), the positive changes social reformers or environmentalists have brought about, the benefits to human life or the maintaining of a better balance between humankind and nature those leading the way in medical or agricultural research have achieved, the good work done by those in different fields of educational development, or the healing as well as meaning and purpose that great works of art and music can have, we see that mediumistic abilities could help us – if we use them rightly – to see into many realms of spirituality.

All these things must surely lead us to a sense of

humility and respect for all life and people, and to consider all as equal and equally valid for different reasons.

We need to understand that every individual and manifestation of life is in fact unique and special – as ultimately sacred – and can have something to offer and enrich our lives.

S: You have studied the lives and teachings of various mystics, lamas and yogis in depth, such as the Dalai Lama, Ramana Maharshi and various Christian mystics. What has this told you about psychic gifts and spirituality as a whole?

GE: That one spills over into the other. That everything can help us to unfold a wider and inclusive view of spirituality and a deeper understanding of ourselves. That what we are is part of a Divine Presence that is in all and transcends all. Many of the teachings I have looked at have awakened within me an ongoing search to discover and find ways that can best unfold That which is beyond boundaries – to what some might describe as miraculous in some traditions. Additionally, they have brought about a growing awakening to how we are capable of great acts of compassion and kindness, and can communicate with and be influenced by realms beyond physical levels of knowing to realising there is an Ultimate Reality permeating all, which is described as the *atman*, the soul, the Spirit, the luminous mind, etc. These are merely terms to describe something which is paradoxically immanent and also transcendent – something that is deathless, sacred and

95

eternal. This takes us beyond the normal seeing, feeling and hearing states of mediumistic and psychic awareness and various miraculous powers, to an understanding of there being a profound Presence within all that is omniscient and omnipotent, and is continuously creating and evolving.

For the Hindu, the Christian, the Muslim, the Sikh and the people of the Jewish faith, it may be termed as God or the Divine. For the Buddhist it will be described as Nirvana, beyond description, forms and concepts, as the state of no mind, pure unconditioned awareness, emptiness, neither being nor non-being, or as the spiritual core of all – our ever-present Buddha Nature.

All of these I believe are interconnected, and can lead us to discovering realms that are beyond physical existence, which can enable us to touch and commune deeply and profoundly with life – both seen and unseen – in more wholesome and balanced ways. Development needs to bring about a realisation and an understanding of the Origin of all things and be at one with It – to live a true state of oneness that recognises that we are not separate from other life and, therefore, spontaneously perform acts of compassion where and whenever possible because of this understanding.

S: What are your views on the general warning made by various wisdom traditions about psychic and supernatural powers being a possible distraction to spiritual life?

GE: On the one hand, seeking mediumistic phenomena

may bring about a spiritual transformation in us and a greater capacity to understand the spiritual nature of our being. The difference lies in our individual intentions and aims. Mediumistic phenomena, whether we are aware of it or not, has at its core the same principles embedded within it as other spiritual practices. But, on the other hand, I think we can become so immersed in looking just at psychic, miraculous and mediumistic aspects that we fail to include these other areas of development. These abilities need to help us to realise that there is something more to life than just the physical realms of existence.

For me, psychic and mediumistic abilities have not only given me an opportunity to communicate with those who have continued their existence after-death of the physical body, but also to view the Cause of all phenomena – to realise that there is That which transcends all and is the Originator, the Preserver and the Creator of all.

If we lose sight of this, I feel, we will be in danger of losing sight of the deeper dimensions of spirituality and any abilities we have will suffer, as we will only be going so far with them and, therefore, placing limits upon them. If we look on psychic, mediumistic and miraculous powers as the pinnacle of spiritual unfoldment, then it seems to me – and I emphasis 'to me' on this point – they would be an obstruction to unfolding other essential facets of our nature.

But people need to arrive at their own views about this matter. We have come a long way from times when people imposed rigid beliefs on others and did not allow them the scope to decide and experience for themselves what was right for them and could give their lives deeper meaning, purpose and direction.

We also need to consider some of the points you have raised for this book, about how such powers are invariably bound-up with a tradition's spiritual path, such as the *siddhis,* which are a part of both the yogic and Buddhist path. Also I should point out again here about mediums I have known that have displayed and developed their abilities to a great level, but their abilities did not change them in anyway that could be called spiritual. Both sides of the coin need to be considered, I feel.

It seems to come down to what we are seeking. If our focus is only on one thing and we are not opening ourselves to other realms of being and awareness, then we are in danger of finding such abilities a distraction to the spiritual whole of unfoldment. It is now recognised that if we develop more than just one type of ability, it enhances others that we have. So we would be limiting mediumistic abilities if we just focus on their development and nothing else. If we are taking a more holistic, integral and inclusive approach, we are hardly in any danger of such powers limiting the 'emergence' (to use a popular term for development) of our spiritual evolution. When one thinks about it, it is a matter of common-sense.

S: What practices have you found helpful for your abilities and how do they affect your daily life?

GE: Meditation in the more traditional sense of the word has certainly enhanced my spiritual awareness and its effects have spilled over into enhancing my mediumship. The use of mantra has affected my psychic and mediumistic awareness. The practice that has come to be known as 'Sitting in the Power', which was given to me through the trance medium Mark Webb, has particularly aided my abilities and benefited other areas of development, because it helps in bringing about an awareness of That Power which is in all. As simple as the practice is, I have found that it leads to an awakening to realms of infinite love that integrates the spirit with our world and can be communicated with, which leads to a realisation that just as human life lives on, so does all life. These practices, I feel, have in many ways enriched my unfoldment and enhanced my spiritual search. But it is not over yet, as the search is an eternal one for us all.

Other practices, which some might not immediately think of as important parts of development, but can help us broaden the abilities we have and take a more holistic approach, involve such things as studying numerous wisdom traditions and spiritual philosophies – which helps to open the mind and bring about an understanding and acceptance of those who hold different beliefs about spirituality – and taking in the creative side of life, including music, art, literature and poetry, and being amongst nature and cultivating a deep awareness of life's interconnectness.

I have found all these things have enhanced my appreciation and sensitivity towards the creative in my own being and the abilities I possess, and a sense of awe and wonder of the Divine that is found in nature – of which human nature and creativity is also a part of – and is the miracle of life itself.

S: Do you have practices for mediumistic unfoldment and others for spiritual development and what advice would you give those who are interested in the development of mediumistic abilities?

GE: Within a Spiritualist context, the answer is 'Yes'. I have over the years sat in a circle with others, and even by myself for mediumistic development, so that the link of the spirit world may build a stronger bond. I am sure different teachers in this field will have their own views about how different areas of development inter-link or can be awakened to.

However, I would like to deal with the practice of attunement with the spirit from the perspective of a medium's awareness. To sit in the stillness and the quietness and invite the spirit world to work with and through us, I think, is important, as the invitation we extend shows a willingness to co-operate with the spirit and what may unfold through this.

Through inviting the spirit to blend with our consciousness and make itself known through our senses, mediumistic abilities can in my experience be brought into being. At first there needs to be this intention of being willing to co-operate, eventually followed by letting this intention and willingness go, allowing our thoughts to become calmer and more settled and adopting an attitude of receptivity to different levels of being.

I think it is important that a developing medium comes to 'truly know' who is working with him or her in the spirit world. By knowing I do not necessarily mean by name or nationality, but learning through the communication that is established, the identity of those working with him or her and begin to recognise how the development of mediumistic abilities influences a medium and how communication shapes itself through his or her individual awareness.

Today there are some who are only interested in quick-fix approaches. There have always been aspects of spiritual, psychic and mediumistic development that can be cultivated quickly. But no matter what field of unfoldment we are looking at, to come to a stage of deeply knowing how different areas of growth work and relate to numerous levels of our being takes time and dedication. It is only through this dedication and deeper knowledge that a true and lasting development is established. Unfortunately some do not wish to study and work deeply with their abilities and see how they can be expanded – how mediumship functions, how contact with different spirit personalities can shape our perceptions and awareness, and the spiritual insight that can come through our unfoldment and the development of these gifts.

Another area for consideration is to do with choice and how to integrate the things that open to us as we move forward, such as a fuller understanding of the spiritual principles and implications behind the communication and how these can widen our perceptions of life and influence our everyday conduct.

If we apply these things we will be able to manifest the potential we have more fully. Practices, such as Sitting in the Power, which help us to expand our mind and consciousness to realms of the seen and unseen, enable us to know for ourselves that the power within us can touch the Power that is in everything – and the more we do this adds to our unfoldment and can bring us to a state of oneness and unity with all.

There is a tremendous amount of data available to us, about people who have undertaken certain practices within their own faith and wisdom traditions – which have brought about different states, through prayer, yogic and Buddhist meditation, mantra and so on – who have experienced other levels of reality and realms of communication. Through such practices, phenomena have manifested of both a mental and physical kind. It is not just through what some may term as 'mediumistic practices' that such things have occurred.

An illustration of what I mean by this can be seen in some of Swami Dharmananda's Hatha yoga students, who have experienced spontaneous awakenings to clairvoyant, clairaudient and clairsentient abilities, which were totally unsought and have come about because of the yogic practices they were doing. It is partly because Swamiji experienced this herself that she investigated some aspects of Spiritualistic phenomena in order to gain a better understanding of what was unfolding in her development.

We need to realise that status, nationality, spiritual backgrounds or beliefs have nothing to do with the phenomena of mediumship. The abilities are a natural part of our being. Except our beliefs will invariably colour our perceptions about it. Our prevalent state of mind and the concepts we possess will condition its manifestation, because of it having to work through the finite physical mind. This is one reason why we need to include other practices, such as those based on spiritual principles and understanding, as they can help us to transcend limiting concepts, beliefs and the world of finite thought and open us more to the Infinite Mind that is present in all and so, help us to grasp more of what the Ultimate Truth of life and eternal existence implies.

Practices that can be found in mediumistic unfold-ment, can be called practices of intention and attention. By applying these two principles to a yearning to know the mysteries of eternal existence and the Truth of our spiritual being, they can bring about a profound awakening to who we really are, why we are here and where we are going on our spiritual journey and an embodiment our authentic nature.

S: Sometimes we hear of healers and mediums giving advice that does not seem helpful. Sometimes with little concern for the consequences of it. There are also times when their information is incorrect. What are your views about these

103

things? How are people meant to approach the advice or information they are given?

GE: These are important questions and ones that need to be looked at openly and frankly, so that we can work towards a mature and practical spirituality that acknowledges possible problems and looks for areas for improvement.

Inaccurate information that may sometimes be given by mediums or healers can lie within their own perceptions and not working enough with their abilities to arrive at a true state of knowing. They might judge things at the time as being correct. But we also have to take into consideration that from one perspective we have a human side to our nature, which is not without its limits and restrictions and can at times affect the quality of mediumistic work. Communicators in the other world tell us that they are also undergoing stages in their evolution, which seems to indicate that they do not necessarily have all the answers and may well be seeing things from perspectives that are not without limitations either.

I think we need to be sensible and realise that our beliefs about, as well as the actions we take in, life are our responsibility. We must reflect upon things that we are told in mediumistic sittings and decide for ourselves what is helpful or not, just as we would with advice given to us in regular life.

Like any ability, there is always room for improvement. Mediumship is by no means a perfect science. Some that communicate with us through mediumship, though their intentions are good, there are times when there are problems in the transmission of the information given. This is why it is important for a medium in all stages of his or her development to be vigilant as to the validity of any information given to them. We ought to inform sitters about any evidence, or information or advise transmitted to them during a sitting, that to the best of our knowledge we feel that what is said is correct, but they should be prepared to accept only that which can be proven as factual.

I think it is essential to realise that the two levels of communication that exist within mediumship are an evolving experience, between the medium who is learning how best to apprehend information coming from the spirit world and this other level of reality learning how best to transmit information to the medium. Every sitting and message is really an experiment with no guarantees. All we can do is see what unfolds and decide for ourselves what is helpful or not.

A particular problem area is our conscious physical mind's perceptions, as we are working with an imperfect instrument – even though the human mind is possibly the most complex mechanism (if we can call it this) in the universe. But perhaps this is why it can at times cause problems. Interestingly, all the great wisdom traditions touch upon teachings about blindness of our True Conscious Nature, so, therefore, our development needs to be about realising the limitations of our finite mind and discovering ways in which it can be better utilised and made a more purer and receptive instrument for the dissemination of Truths.

The mediumistic journey is in many ways multi-faceted and needs to be open to evolvement at all times. Yet because of evolvement, it means there will be times when new ways of working unfold, which we will be unfamiliar with. I remember you shared some experiences in the first book we wrote together about how you once were aware of some images subjectively that could at first be interpreted in a certain way – as they actually appeared – but they needed to be probed to arrive at their true meaning, as they were symbolic representations of people's surnames. If information was given as first perceived, it would not have been accurate. It shows how we have to work with mediumistic impressions, instead of being quick to say what one is first perceiving to be true.

We, therefore, need to check any impression or information received for its validity and consider how best to transmit it to those that would be the recipients of it. This I feel is why mediums need to include honesty and integrity in their development, as I believe these will affect the fruits of their work.

S: On the one hand, some people might think being in touch with spirit people as a bit strange. On the other hand, these same people might consider being in touch with Divinity as more of a natural experience. What would you say to such people?

GE: We cannot separate the spirit world from the Divine, as everything is interrelated. If, as I believe, all life survives and is interconnected, then why should it appear strange to commune and be in contact with different realms of existence? In all the great wisdom traditions this contact with other realms has been mentioned and has at various times throughout history to the present day been practiced. In some traditions people who walked this earth have come to be revered as saints, gods or goddesses and there are accounts of communication with these people in non-physical after-death states.

We also need to consider how throughout the ages ancestor worship has been intrinsically bound-up with many traditions (even to this day), how there are accounts about those that have been described as angelic beings communicating with various people, and how people have prayed to different individuals, such as saints, as they are seen as intercessors before God who will act on people's behalf. There are also shamans and oracles who are consulted in various traditions and many renowned mystics have displayed mediumistic types of abilities.

It seems to me that there has always existed in humankind's psyche the belief in non-physical realms of existence. Early indigenous people and shamans were the first to connect with a spirit world permeating nature and to communicate with their departed ancestors. Others have looked towards the more transcendent areas of spirituality. Although there are some who have never completely separated themselves from some of the early indigenous beliefs and practices, there are some who have, which has led to an unhealthy separation between nature and the Spirit. All areas need to be included in the search for the One Ultimate Reality that expresses Itself in and through all.

If we accept that life is eternal and there are other realms of existence intertwined with our physical world, then it must surely be a natural step in our evolution to be able to commune with these other realms and with those who are living on. We need to recognise that there are different ways in which to approach the many-faceted dimensions of spirituality, and be open to all areas that can lead us to healthier states of spiritual being and embrace the all-ness of what eternal life is about.

Appendix 2
A Conversation with Glyn Edwards on Spirituality

S: Who has particularly impressed you and why?

GE: Ramana Maharshi is one of many. His central teaching was based around the age-old question 'Who am I?' which obviously leads to self-enquiry and can help us put aside any doctrines or distractions that inhibit our unfoldment. Out of asking himself this simple question there arose a natural goodness within him that embraced all people, irrespective of their individual beliefs, theories or backgrounds.

I have also been drawn to the ideals and life of Mahatma Gandhi, who sought a peaceful settlement without violence, as well the Dalai Lama, who has also trod a similar path. These two spiritual giants have endeavoured to live by the principles of their beliefs and have in many ways changed the world in which we live – showing us by example, ways that we can truly be and the power of individual and collective non-violent action, which highlights a central tenet of spirituality. They have both showed us that the only solution to all the conflicts of human nature is to love and care compassionately for one another – a core teaching that goes back to Jesus, the Hebrew Bible, the Buddha and many influential yogis and yoginis and spiritual teachings.

There are numerous other people and writers that have inspired me, such as Sri Aurobindo and M. P. Pandit (who we were fortunate enough to meet), for their practical and integral approach to development and Earnest Holmes for his profound common-sense about spirituality.

S: You have just touched on the next question, which is what do you see as the most important thing or things on the spiritual path and can you give reasons for why you think it or they are important?

GE: As well as what has been said, other facets of importance are about having determination, dedication and a mind that is receptive to the creative and wholesome possibilities of what can unfoldment in our life.

Although others may touch our lives and guide us, we are responsible for our individual unfoldment. As we enter into development with an open mind and a willingness to grow into spiritual maturity – which means including the inevitable difficulties and suffering we and others encounter, along with blissful moments of awakening to Divinity – we begin to realise that all life is ultimately One; that there is no clear division between set systems of belief, or everyday life and spiritual understanding.

Behind all there is That which is Creative – the same Spirit is in all – which has imbued all life with the ability to express Its Creativity, to become co-Creators, and has allowed humanity to discover life's true purpose and meaning: that ultimately everything is ruled by love and that our True Nature is ultimately loving.

S: In life there are often various crossroads to face and it can be difficult at times to know the right path or action to take. Is there any advice someone who is highly intuitive like yourself can give about this?

GE: Deep intuitive wisdom that can guide us in the right actions in life takes time and patience to develop and requires us to cultivate various powers, such as reflective reasoning, knowledge based on experience and an acceptance of things as they really are.

Life is always about moving on and evolving in the eternity of existence, and each of us needs to face each moment, each passing phase of life with wisdom, acceptance and compassionate understanding. We are all imbued with intuitive abilities, but we need wisdom and compassion as well in order to be able to reflect and learn from the actions of, and various situations encountered in, life in skilful ways and find paths in which our actions can benefit not only ourselves, but also others.

There is no point in living with regrets if things have not turned out as we feel they should, as the past has gone and the only thing that can be changed about it is how we respond to and are influenced by it in the present. There also needs to be an awareness of and a creative responsiveness to what new events and undiscovered potential may unfold. We are infinite, and because we are infinite we obviously have no beginning or end. Our beginning-less and endless Self does not need to view life as missed opportunities, but seeks to call us to ways in which it can skilfully manifest its True Nature – its Divinity – more purely in every moment.

S: Some have ideas about spiritual people being very placid and taking life's problems lying down. Yet we find people, such as Matthew Fox, who is probably one of the most influential teachers around at the moment, mentioning in his autobiography how he sent a seventy page document to someone who underhandedly tried to stop his ordination being accepted – even though the person was unsuccessful anyway – and people, such as William Wilberforce, Martin Luther King Jr. and Mahatma Gandhi hardly seemed inactive when it came to matters of injustice and inequality. What are your views?

GE: The part of us that believes in justice needs to express itself. Some Christians even go as far to condone what they see as 'righteous anger', which is different to an immature, self-centred childish anger that arises because an individual cannot have his or her own way.

Spirituality embraces actions that can bring about positive changes where and whenever possible. To think of the Divine and spiritual development as purely transcendent and overlook the immanent, omnipresent, feminine and creative aspects of Its sacredness has arguably lead us to our current state of destroying the Earth and not caring enough about a balanced life, injustice, inequality and poverty. I know that this is something you have also taught and have touched upon in your book with Swami Dharmananda.

It seems to me to be about the age-old quest for finding a balance between doing and being – a development of an awareness of things as they are and states of equanimity, along with an affirmation of life, rather than an escape from it. Although suffering exists and physical life is transient and forever undergoing change, it does not mean that we should not take part and find meaning and purpose in life – even at the risk of displaying our human qualities. Life on Mother Earth is not some totally dark realm that we feel we would be only too pleased to escape from.

Yes, there have always been those who have retreated from life and there are many arguments for and against this. But to make an ideal about spiritual people being placid leaves out much of what spirituality is about. We find the Buddha choosing a middle path and many notable mystics in charge of monasteries and/or religious communities, such as Hildegard of Bingen and St Teresa of Avila, which when you read about their lives you see that their positions required them to make difficult choices and sometimes take a definite stand for what they saw as fair and just.

If we study the lives and biographies of some of the great masters of spirituality – those that have brought about great changes or have profoundly influenced people's lives – no matter how advanced we might consider them to be, we ought to never lose sight of the fact that they still have human qualities. ("Keep me away from the wisdom which does not cry, the philosophy which does not laugh …", the mystical poet Kahlil Gibran said.) Invariably, they are not people who could be described as placid, but have been people of action, social change and profound teachings. It is their sense of humanity and human justice that often spurred them on to do great things and impart exceptional wisdom.

Some have even displayed outbursts of anger about injustice that has driven them to bring about positive changes in the world and others have possessed what might be described as all-too-human weaknesses. But in spite of such weaknesses, it does not undermine the work they have done. It shows us how the spiritual path is not always easy. I noticed in one of Matthew Fox's books on one of the most important Christian thinkers in history, St Thomas Aquinas [*Sheer Joy: Conversations with Thomas Aquinas on Creation Spirituality*], that he wrote about him having clay feet and sees nothing wrong with this.

Our human nature and character is bound-up with our individual personality, which does not necessarily imply being unhealthily ego-centred, as some mistakenly believe (ego and personality are different things), as we can have a healthy spiritual-centred personality just as much as an unhealthy ego-centred one, of which there are numerous important realms of unfoldment between the two.

Sometimes we think of spirituality in terms of idealistic routes of expression, which do not allow for the complexities of existence and the many different facets of a person's life. There is often a problem of placing people we admire on pedestals, as we invariably becoming disheartened when they do not live up to the unfair projections we place on them, which probably no one could live up to.

We can also beat ourselves up when we do not live up to unrealistic ideals we impose on ourselves. There are often reasons why we act less than we feel we should. This is why great teachers, such as Jesus, taught that we should not judge lest we be judged [Matt. 7:1]. "Never judge someone until you have walked a thousand miles in his or her shoes", as the saying goes.

Let us allow others to be as they are and to follow their own paths of evolution − physically, emotionally, mentally, morally and spiritually. Although I believe that at an ultimate level of reality we are not human beings unfolding to spiritual experience, but spiritual beings experiencing human realms of existence. To me, this points to something that is within human experience which is evolving through the activity of a spiritual Force within us and in all life in the universe. It indicates, as previously mentioned, that development is about learning how to overcome all sense of separation from our True Nature.

We should never lose sight of the fact that the Spirit within all is constantly seeking to refine the finite and to express Itself more purely through it. This is why unfoldment, awareness, compassion and wisdom are key areas of spirituality, as they lead us to more purer states of being, knowing and acting in everyday life.

S: *People sometimes take the stand that spirituality is not about traditional wisdom and study, but about their own experiences. What do you think about this?*

GE: I can understand why some might feel the need to reject traditional religious ideas and want to discard any investigation into them, as there are areas that need to be re-evaluated and made more relevant to our current age. But we have to be careful of throwing the baby out with the bath water. To rely purely on individual experience without other areas of development can make it hard for us to know how to apply, embody and integrate experiences, as well as have the language to even talk about and understand them and, therefore, share our experiences with others.

I remember you telling me about some of the work you did in schools, where some children as young as eleven responded positively to learning terms and language which enabled them to talk openly about spiritual experiences. As adults we can have resistance to learning new things, but if we truly wish to grow we need to overcome our resistances and explore the real issues behind them.

However, to follow a path of purely intellectual study without some personal insight and experience is also not the best route. It needs to be a balance of the two. There is much in our unfoldment that requires some points of reference. To ignore the writings and teachings of both the past and present is to ignore the evolution of our spiritual brothers and sisters and the insights they have had about everyone's spiritual development. We will obviously have to be discerning with what we study, and this too is an important practice and part of the process of spiritual unfoldment.

There is of course a need to base our moving forward on our experiences, but there is also a need to constantly reflect upon how our experiences are affecting our beliefs and overall growth into a True Selfhood that embraces all. It is clear that on one level religious experiences can separate and divide people into different camps where they feel they have the only Truth and that others have somehow got it wrong. This is why it is important to study, widen our understanding, find common ground, respect others' beliefs and realise that we are all in our own individual way searching for That which Ultimately Unites us – a Supreme non-separate Reality.

There is also the fact that no one person can know everything and there have been those in various traditions that have looked at different areas of spirituality that are essential and can help us, and from which we can draw much food for thought, such as matters concerning modern ethical dilemmas, political and social change, physical and psychological benefits of various practices, and so on.

We must realise the Light that shines through other faiths, other ways of thinking and traditions. An open mind to others is essential. If one is considering spirituality from a mediumistic perspective, one ought to consider what the spirit world is ultimately about. Is it not all-encompassingly bound-up with all traditions, life, creativity, evolution and people and, most importantly, with those trying to help humanity realise its spiritual nature and compassionate potential?

Combining insights and teachings of the past and present, along with personal experience, can spur us on to discover deeper and more valid universal Truths, with the hope that what we find, embody, live-out and share, will benefit others we walk with on the path.

S: Finally, although much of what you have said could be seen to cover this question, can you summarise what spirituality means to you, as it can mean different things to different people. On the one hand, some teachers and writers think of spiritual realms of development as being about mystical union or deep states of meditation. On the other hand, if we are using the word to describe anyone who has a natural sense of goodness about them and about wholesome development and actions in daily life, we are obviously using the word in a much broader way.

GE: Yes, it can be used to mean different things. For me it is about an embracing of all people, life and nature – to truly see and value the good in all traditions and in different forms of wisdom. It is bound-up with realising that the same Supreme Spirit exists in all – that the activity of the psychic, mediumistic and miraculous, and the phenomena which comes from these, must never restrict the potential for spirituality, spiritual awareness and the recognition of equality, or restrict practices of kindness, natural goodness and compassionate actions.

How can we judge that a carpenter or stonemason

may not just through his or her work develop profound spiritual qualities and become a great spiritual influence to others who come to know him or her and his or her work. Additionally, are cathedrals and temples not built by such people whose names we rarely know? Who are we to say that an agnostic is not a spiritual person? Or are we seeking to impose a set system of belief that excludes certain people from its club because they do not hold the same views and practices as we do?

Let us realise that spirituality is more than just meditation practices, rituals, beliefs and personal experiences; it encompasses the all-ness of life. Neither is it a truth that only a few possess, or a philosophy which makes us stand coldly separate from life.

Because some have gifts, such as insight into other worlds that are seen to connect with ours, or the ability to heal, we should not consider that these set them apart from others or indicate that they are more advanced or important than anyone else. Everyone has within them the potential for the same Divine qualities, which can be brought to the surface at any point in their lives. Sometimes we may be unaware that we are entertaining angels (meaning anyone who displays natural goodness), as the New Testament passage reminds us – and is one of many reasons why we need to consider showing kindness to strangers [Heb. 13:2] – such as when someone listens to our troubles and truly empathises with us. Is this not as valid a spiritual act as any that we can think of? True and spontaneous selfless acts of kindness and compassion are really the core of spirituality.

It is time that all of us, no matter what tradition, or none, took a step back and reviewed what is meant by spirituality. Although mediumistic awareness can be seen as a natural part of our being, just as breathing and kindness is, it is only a facet of the whole. Let us apply the principles of what we may term as higher living. This is not about seeing ourselves as more advanced than others, or separate or aloof from everyday life, but about manifesting our greatest gifts and recognising that there is goodness in all people, including ourselves, even though our human nature can get in the way of displaying it at times, as the symbol of *ying* and *yang* reminds us with the white spot in the black and the black in the white – reminding us that no person is entirely perfect, as equally as there is no one who is entirely bad.

We need to cultivate an understanding and a state of being that accepts and loves others and ourselves, and realises that our True Nature is endeavouring to help us to awaken to the reality of what spirituality is and how to live deeply and skilfully by it in every moment. In looking into ourselves for the greatest gifts we possess, we discover the gifts of wisdom and Self-knowledge, which are the gateways to freedom, true peace and enlightenment. They help us to find unity in diversity and the Compassionate Spirit in all.

Glossary

After-death States – various wisdom traditions mention having knowledge of different realms of existence encountered after death of the physical body.

Allah – the Islamic word for God.

Apports – objects that are materialised with the aid of a physical medium and the spirit world.

Astral – a non-physical psychic realm where the physical body is sometimes said to have a double (an astral body). In Hinduism, the astral and subtle realms are interchangeable terms.

Astral Projection – the ability to expand one's awareness to non-physical realms of consciousness. Some believe in an astral body having the ability to travel to other realms and places. The idea of astral projection has been around for thousands of years and can be found in ancient Chinese beliefs.

Atman (Self) – the eternal True Self in Hindu spirituality that can be seen as individual, universal and transcendent and connects with the Ultimate Ground of all (see Brahman).

Attunement – the ability to blend/attune one's awareness with psychic, spiritual or mediumistic states of consciousness. It functions in numerous ways, such as how we relate to nature, with all life and the many aspects of the Divine within us and in all things.

Aura – different levels of energy surrounding the physical body, which are connected with numerous facets of one's being: the physical,

121

emotional, mental, spiritual, etc.

Authentic/True Nature or Self – the part of our being that is Divine and connects with all. It can be viewed as having an individual, universal and ultimate transcendent facet to it, which has the power to harmonise conflicting parts into a synthesised and sacred whole, and help us to find unity with all. Modern psychology also uses these terms, but will not necessarily relate them with the Divine. Branches of Buddhism use the term 'Buddha Nature' instead of authentic or True Self.

Bhakti Yoga (devotion/love) – a devotional path towards the Divine or towards a teacher as a manifestation of the Divine.

Bilocation – an ability to appear in two places at the same time.

Brahman – in Hindu spirituality it is the One Ultimate Reality within and beyond the many forms of the universe.

Buddha (one who is awake) – someone who is enlightened and has woken up to the Truth and is seeing things clearly and as they really are. It also refers to the historical Buddha.

Buddha Nature – there are two aspects to it: developable and naturally abiding within us. It transcends thought, is thoroughly pure, undefiled, empty of all dualities and experienced as a joyous expansiveness with infinite positive potential.

Chakra (wheel) – a principal energy centre in the psychic/subtle body.

Channelling – a term sometimes used to describe spiritual teachings given through a medium while in a trance-like state.

Chi – in Taoism it is the vital and primordial energy and life force, the cosmic spirit that pervades and gives life to all things.

Clairaudience / Clairsentience / Clairvoyance – The ability to see (clairvoyance), hear (clairaudience) or feel (clairsentience) the Divine, discarnate spirit personalities or things of a psychic nature, either subjectively or objectively, has existed in all the great wisdom traditions, indigenous and tribal traditions through-out the ages. They have been viewed by many great masters of spirituality as being natural abilities, which can be awakened through spiritual practices, such as meditation, contemplative prayer and yoga exercises, whether one is consciously trying to develop them or not. Yoga refers to them as the *siddhis*. The Buddha taught about developing the Divine Ear and the Divine Eye, and seeing into past lives and the reasons why people suffer and are reborn. Clairaudient, clairsentient and clairvoyant abilities are also found in Christian mysticism and have been displayed by numerous saints. The word clairvoyance is sometimes employed to refer to mediumship in a general way by the media and in the public arena.

Collective Unconscious – a universal interconnected consciousness acting within the Cosmos. Carl Jung believed it housed powerful archetypes and memories which can be traced back to the beginnings of human thought.

Consciousness – to have a level of self-awareness. In spiritual traditions consciousness is not seen to rely on just the physical body for its existence and is often viewed as functioning in numerous ways, such as on an individual and universal level, as well as in Ultimate Transcendent states of mystical experience.

Contemplation – can simply refer to reflecting on life and one's experiences. In Christian mysticism it is a form of prayer that is comparable to yogic and Buddhist forms of meditation.

Cosmic Intelligence or Cosmic/Universal Consciousness – a creative interconnected mind that came into being with the Creation of the universe, of which we are all a unique part of, which can be realised in transcendent states of consciousness.

Creation Centred Spirituality – a spirituality which looks for ways to become co-Creators with the Divine and find harmony with the Creative Mind of the universe. Its roots can be found in the Christian mystical tradition, and in Tantra, connected with various *chakras* and with Shakti (the Creative Divine Mother energy), and with aspects of Sufi, Buddhist, Taoist, ancient Celtic, African, Australian Aboriginal, Native American and Hasidic Jewish spirituality. The visionary activist Matthew Fox has done much to promote the teachings of Creation Spirituality over the last few decades.

Dark Night of the Soul – a period of spiritual dryness that is seldom lit by any uplifting spiritual experience. But, nonetheless, it is invariably seen as a stage of progression on the spiritual path.

Development Circle – a gathering of people who meet in order to develop spiritual, mediumistic and psychic gifts and abilities. The origins could *possibly* be traced back to indigenous practices of sitting in a sacred space represented by a circle and the saying of Jesus about two or three people gathering in his name.

Dhikr – a word used by Sufis meaning 'remembrance' and refers to the practice of remembering God often.

Direct Voice Phenomena – refers to a form of physical mediumship where the voice of a discarnate spirit personality is made physically audible.

Divine – an Ultimate Sacred Interconnectedness, which works and is universally present within our cosmos and also transcends it.

Dukkha (unsatisfactoriness) – one of three marks of existence in Buddhism. It is often translated as 'suffering' into English, but the word 'unsatisfactoriness' is now seen as a more accurate translation.

Ecozoic Age – a phase of the Earth's history requiring humans to live at one with its needs and finding mutually beneficial enrichment.

Ectoplasm – a substance that is said to be a mixture of physical and non-physical material used in physical mediumistic phenomena by the spirit world in order to materialise individual spirit personalities and physical objects (apports). Other traditions may have connections with this area, such as some of the phenomena witnessed around the lives of various saints. However, further investigation is still needed before we can say for sure.

Ecumenical – a seeking for unity and mutual respect amongst the world's religious traditions.

Ego – it can have different interpretations. In mystical and Eastern wisdom it refers to our individual sense of self, to self-centredness and how we see ourselves as separate from other life.

Enlightenment – a state of being where one has woken-up to seeing and embodying the Ultimate Truth, although different traditions and branches of faith have various views about it.

Etheric Energy – comparable with *prana* and *chi* energy, and seen as a vital energy working in and surrounding the body and as a universal life-force.

Fana – a word used by Sufis meaning 'passing away', and refers to dying to the world and finding survival in God.

Global Spirituality – spirituality concerned with global issues.

Grace – a blessing and/or gift from God that helps a seeker move forward in his or her evolvement. Life and Creation itself are also seen as gifts from God and, therefore, part of God's grace in traditions such as Christianity and Judaism and some devotional schools of Hinduism. Arguably, the concept of grace is not in the historical Buddha's teachings, whereas later in different strands of Mahayana Buddhism a form of grace that helps spiritual seekers starts to come in.

Guides/Spirit Guides – discarnate spirit personalities that are believed to interact with the physical world and aid people's development.

Guides/Spiritual Guides – people who help others in their spiritual growth, such as a guru in the yogic tradition.

Guru (teacher) – can refer either to a spiritual teacher who dispels darkness or to the Divine/God as the Supreme Guru.

Hatha Yoga (yoga of force) – a branch of yoga that places emphasis on physical postures, cleansing techniques and breathing exercises.

Healer – someone who heals with the interaction of the spirit world, or through the use of prayer or affirmations, or anyone who can restore someone to a state of well-being through a variety of methods, such as naturopathic remedies, holistic practices, acupuncture, or the laying-on of hands at an Evangelical meeting.

Higher Self – a part of us which houses our finest attributes and qualities, such as compassion, kindness and wisdom.

Holiness – a state of being near to God, being holy or made whole.

Holistic (Wholistic) – including and harmonising the whole self: the body, feelings, emotions, mind and spiritual levels of being.

'I'/the 'I' – the individual self that we see as separate from other people and things, which has associations with the ego (self-centredness). It should be noted that Western psychology has many different theories about the ego.

'I'/the True 'I' Consciousness – the Ultimate Self/Reality (a non-separate Reality).

Illumination – mystical visions, experiences and openings of the mind and consciousness.

Immanent – when used to refer to the Divine, it refers to the Divine as being ever-present.

Integral Spirituality – a spirituality that includes many traditions, disciplines, insights and practices of both the East and West, such as modern science and psychology, and Eastern philosophy and practices, and looks for an integration of the spiritual whole of our individual, social and universal selves.

Integral Yoga – a synthesised path of self-discovery and expression formulated by Sri Aurobindo: a unitive path of perfection, bhakti (devotion), jnana (insight and knowledge) and karma (action) yoga, which aims for a spiritual purification and transformation of the complete personality.

Interconnectedness (non-separateness) – that everything shares an interrelationship.

Inter-faith – a seeking for an open dialogue, and an acceptance of difference and finding of common ground between different faiths.

Interspirituality – a contemporary term for inter-faith, which seeks to overcome barriers between different faiths and incorporate practices and insights from different traditions.

Intuition – the ability to know information without the aid of the physical senses. In spiritual literature intuition is often associated with wisdom and profound levels of insight, but it can function in everyday levels of knowing about something being right or wrong, or everyday hunches.

Intuitive – an alternative word for someone who is mediumistic and/or psychic. It has many links with intuition (see above).

Jnana Yoga (yoga of knowledge) – yogic path to freedom via wisdom, discernment and intuitive insight.

Kabbalah – a mystical branch of the Jewish wisdom tradition.

Karma (action) – refers to 'actions having consequences' and the will, which, therefore, have an effect on one's spiritual progress, in either a positive or negative way, in this life or a future one.

Karma Yoga (yoga of action) – a path that leads to spiritual liberation through skilful willed actions.

Kundalini Yoga (yoga of psychic energy) – a path that seeks liberation through the use of creative psychic energy.

Liberation – freedom from psychological states and worldly conditioning which restrict the true spiritual nature of our being.

Lower Self – part of our being that is in disharmony with its True Spiritual Nature.

Mandala (circle) – circular design representing the universe and a particular deity.

Mantra Yoga – the repetition of mantras as a path to liberation. Words, sounds or short affirmations are repeated in order to affirm an aspect of the Divine, which is invariably represented by the name of a specific deity. In Mahayana Buddhism mantras are often used for bringing about an awakening to spiritual qualities within oneself and insights into the Ultimate Nature of existence.

Maya – can have many meanings, such as the Ultimate Creative Power

127

9

in the universe or the world of 'illusion' or 'delusion' in Hindu spirituality. It can also be interpreted as 'misconceptions'.

Meditation – can imply many different types of practices. In Christian spirituality meditation can refer to visualisation and more reflective practices. In the yogic tradition it can be about focusing one's attention on an object, or on the breath or on a mantra. The contemporary Christian Meditation Movement, founded by the English Benedictine monk John Main, promoted yogic forms of meditation, such as mantra and various breathing exercises.

Mediumship – the ability to see, hear or feel spirit personalities that no longer have a physical existence. Additionally, trance and physical mediumship and healers who are aided by spirit personalities are other areas that fall under this heading. The word literally refers to someone who is in the middle of two realms of existence and acts as a mediator between the two.

Mind/Higher Mind – a wide term, which has connections with the discriminating faculty and the rational mind (the intellect), as well as wisdom and insight.

Mind/Lower Mind – automatic functions of the mind and sensory perceptions.

Mind/Unconscious Mind (individual unconscious) – levels of the mind that we are not consciously aware of, which include instinctual drives and memories of all past experiences that can affect our personality on a conscious level. The spiritual, psychic and psychological implications of an unconscious mind are vast, as it cannot only be seen to link with parts of ourselves that carry subliminal influences that affect our conduct, but also with the collective unconscious mind that links with all things in the universe.

Moksha (liberation) – freedom from conditioned worldly existence.

Monism – the belief in there being ultimately only One Reality behind the many forms of life and matter in the universe (both seen and unseen).

Morphogenetic Fields – a biological field permeating nature, which contains information to shape the exact form of living things, as well as its behaviour. Cambridge biologist Rupert Sheldrake is particularly known for this theory, and has comparisons with Carl Jung's theory of the Collective Unconscious. It has many psychic and religious implications concerning an interconnected creative and psychic mind working within nature.

Mudra (seal) – a hand or whole body gesture used in meditation. It includes invoking an opening of awareness while doing the mudra, such as a realisation of one's spiritual nature, or the joining of individual consciousness with the omnipresent and transcendent Divine Consciousness.

Mystic – a person who seeks through meditation or contemplative prayer to attain unity with the Divine.

Mystical Experience – a wide variety of experiences are often placed under this heading, but a true mystical experience would imply having an experience of union or oneness with the Divine.

Mysticism – a life of prayer and/or meditation, work and discipline dedicated to serving and finding unity with the Divine.

Myths – Myths or legends about heroic struggles or personal sacrifice can be seen as powerful archetypes – as symbolic metaphors for the spiritual journey. Joseph Campbell found many myths that were common to all wisdom traditions, which tell important stories about the spiritual seeker's individual search for Truth and his or her return home.

Near-death Experiences – spiritual, religious and out-of-body experiences people have had when they have almost died.

Nirvana – a state of enlightenment achieved in meditation practices.

Non-attachment – it is essential to understand that non-attachment is not about being aloof and separate from life. Just as we would not consider the cure of an illness as being about taking medicine that merely numbs our feelings and physical senses and makes us unaware of any pain. Non-attachment encompasses acknowledgment of and being unbound by any restrictive feeling or mental state.

Non-dualism (non-separateness) – the belief that while all things appear to have an individual uniqueness, everything interconnects with an underlying unity (see Monism).

Omnipotent – all-powerful.

Omnipresence – everywhere and in everything.

Omniscient – all-knowing.

Oneness – a state of being in harmony with all things.

Out-of-Body Experience – an experience where one's consciousness seems to leave the physical body.

Pantheism – the belief in a Divinity that is present in all things.

Panentheism – the belief in a Divinity that is present in all things in the universe and beyond. An omnipresent and transcendent Divinity.

Perennial Wisdom – a belief that underlying all the great wisdom traditions there is a universal truth running through them.

Physical Phenomena – an area of mediumship which deals with how the spirit world can bring about materialisations of spirit personalities, dematerialise physical objects and re-materialise them again, or recreate the audible voice of a spirit personality.

Pluralism – theologically implies there being more than one principle at work in the universe.

Pranayama – the practice of overcoming limitations of the body and mind through the use of *pranic*/psychic energy, particularly with the aid of breathing exercises.

Prayer – there are many forms of prayer. For example, some Christian practices of contemplative prayer are comparable to Eastern practices of meditation. Other forms of prayer can include affirmations, reflecting on sacred texts or asking for Divine help.

Projection – negative parts of our character that are denied and projected onto others.

Psyche – the inner instrument through which we think, feel and discriminate. It consists of the lower, higher and unconscious mind and the individual sense of self.

Psychic – someone who has the ability to know things without the aid of the physical senses, or something that cannot be explained by accepted laws of science. The word also refers to psychological levels of being and levels connected with the unconscious mind.

Psychic Abilities – different traditions have called psychic abilities by different names, such as the *siddhis* in Hindu yoga, in which the ultimate *siddhi* is the realisation of one's True Nature and liberation from restrictive states of existence.

Psychometry – the ability to psychically feel into physical objects and obtain information connected with the object.

Quantum Theory – an area of science that studies the laws of physics that are happening on a very small scale. Of particular interest in this field is the discovery that on a sub-atomic level there is no clear separation between people, objects and other phenomena – that there is an ultimate interconnectedness between all.

Qur'an – the holy book of the Islamic tradition.

Reincarnation – the belief that after-death the soul is reborn into another physical body, or into another realm, such as the heavenly realm, or the realm of hungry ghosts or fighting demons, as mentioned in the Buddhist tradition. But it should be noted that these realms can also be interpreted as different psychological states of being that we slip in and out of numerous times a day.

Sacred – that which embodies the truth of a religion or an aspect of Divinity and is, therefore, something to be in awe of, as well as revered, respected and cherished because of its preciousness.

Saint – another word for a holy person; someone who is seen as virtuous and lives or lived in the Divine's presence.

Samadhi – the climax of yogic meditation practices where one realises the True Self.

Samsara – the world of conditioned existence in the physical world,

131

which is tied-up with ideas about the continual cycle of lives:
birth, death and rebirth. It is seen as a world of unsatisfactoriness
that we reinforce individually and collectively with our minds and
beliefs, which do not show us how things really are.

Seer – someone who has visions of a prophetic nature and/or can
perceive things beyond physical realms of existence.

Self-awareness – to be conscious of one's inner feelings, thoughts,
emotions, desires, motives, exterior actions and one's True Self.

Self-realisation – to realise one's full potential and/or one's relationship
with the Divine.

Shadow/the Shadow – the parts of ourselves that we do not accept and
are often hard for us to own.

Shakti (power/force) – the Ultimate Reality in its creative and female
aspect, which acts in the universe. It is also connected with
Kundalini yoga.

Shaman – someone who has the ability to contact and enter into the
spirit world.

Skilfulness – the ability to be spiritually creative in everyday life and
conduct ourselves in a manner that brings about balanced living.

Socially Engaged Spirituality – a spirituality that seeks to bring about
beneficial changes in society and the world.

Soul – a wide term that can mean different things to different people.
For some it is looked upon as the same as the individual spark of
the spirit in all; for others, it can be associated more with the
psychological self.

Spirit – can have many different meanings, such as one's individual
spirit, or used as a plural to refer those who no longer have a
physical existence. It can also be used as another word for the
Divine and the sacredness of all.

Spirit World – can refer to an interconnected reality that permeates all,
a spiritual existence, or a world that is inhabited by individual
spirit personalities.

132

Sub-conscious – sometimes used as an alternative word for the unconscious mind, or to describe thoughts, feelings and actions that are just beneath surface levels of awareness, which can be accessed by the conscious mind – termed the 'preconscious' by Sigmund Freud.

Subtle Body – a psychic body mentioned in different traditions that can include the *chakras* and different elements (earth, fire, water, air and ether) and energies, as well as emotional and mental realms.

Sufism – a mystical branch of Islam.

Superconsciousness – has associations with different states, such as hearing astral sounds, seeing visions and experiencing cosmic energy, which can lead to a realisation of the Divine's omnipresent and transcendent nature. Such things can be seen as being higher and lower levels of superconsciousness, which can lead to an opening to one's authentic spiritual nature.

Surrender (letting go and letting God) – the practice of letting go of the individual will and handing one's thoughts, ideas and actions over to the Divine or to more spiritual states of consciousness.

Synchronicity – random events that take on symbolic meaning, such as a bird flying into a room signifying bad news, or natural coincidental events that are seen as miraculous happenings.

Tantra (continuity) – refers to Tantra yoga and its teachings, which focus on the use of *shakti* energy.

Tapas (heat) – refers to austerity, which may be done for the purpose of overcoming the body and purifying oneself. The word was also used to refer to psychic powers in early yogic teachings.

Torah – a wide term that includes God's law as revealed to Moses.

Trance – a wide term, which can refer to deep mystical states where one is not aware of the exterior world, or to different types of mediumistic phenomena, where a spirit personality can control a medium's or Spiritualist healer's consciousness and actions. But it should be noted, that there are different and subtle degrees in which this is said to happen. For example, a medium might be entranced by a spirit personality, but still be aware of and influence aspects of what is being said and happening.

Transcendent – levels beyond normal physical experience.

Transfiguration – to be transformed into a pure spiritual state of being. In Christianity it also refers to the account of Jesus appearing in radiant glory to three of his disciples. As a Spiritualistic phenomena it is associated with changes brought about in a medium's facial appearance in order to take on physical characteristics of a discarnate spirit personality.

Transpersonal – states of consciousness beyond the boundaries of personal identity.

Unfoldment – a similar word to development, which refers more to the removal of things that stop us from recognising and manifesting our True Spiritual Nature. Unfolding authentic qualities and wisdom and working towards a spiritual synthesis that influences the whole of our lives.

Unitive Consciousness – in Christian mysticism it is where the Ultimate Mystery is realised and the seeker recognises his or her co-relationship with the Creator. A non-separate consciousness.

Visionary – in spiritual traditions it can refer to someone who has prophetic gifts or teaches profound wisdom about the future.

Wholism – including and working on the spiritual whole of our existence; from the body, mind and emotions, and the realms of individual, social and global spirituality, to Cosmological spirituality.

World/Earth-centric – concerned with global issues.

Yahweh – Hebrew word for God.

Yantra (devise) – a geometric design that represent one's individual self and a particular deity. It is used for meditation purposes and realising one's Ultimate Nature.

Yoga (to yoke/to bind and make whole) – the most popular forms are bhakti, karma and jnana in Hinduism. Yoga is also practiced in the Buddhist and Jain traditions.

Bibliography

Abhayananda, S, *Mysticism and Science: A Call for Reconciliation*, O Books, Winchester and New York, 2007.

Affifi, A. E., *The Mystical Philosophy of Mhyid Din-Ibnul 'Arabi*, SH Muhammad Ashraf, Lahore, 1979.

Arberry, Arthur J. (translator), *The Koran*, Oxford University Press, Oxford, 1983 (reprint).

— , *Sufism: An Account of the Mystics of Islam*, Unwin Paperbacks, London, 1979.

Aurobindo, Sri, *Record of Yoga: Volume 2*, Sri Aurobindo Ashram Publication Department, Pondicherry, 2001.

— , and the Mother, *The Psychic Being: Soul: Its Nature , Mission and Evolution*, Sri Aurobindo Ashram, Pondicherry, 2003 (reprint).

— , *The Yoga of Sleep and Dreams: The Night-School of Sadhana* (compiled with an introduction by A. S. Dalal), Sri Aurobindo Ashram, Pondicherry, 2004.

Baldick, Julian, *Mystical Islam: An Introduction to Sufism*, I. B. Tauris and Co. Ltd., London, 1992 (reprint).

Benson, Herbert, *Mind/Body Interaction – including Tibetan Studies*, chapter three in *Mind Science: An East West Dialogue* (edited by Goleman and Thurman), Wisdom, Boston, 1991.

Berry, Thomas, *Evening Thoughts: Reflecting on Earth as Sacred Community* (edited by Mary Evelyn Tucker), Sierra Book Club, San Francisco, 2006.

Bodhi, Bihikkhu, *In the Buddha's Words: An Anthology of Discourses from the Pali Canon*, Wisdom Books, Boston, 2005.

Bowker, John, *The Complete Bible Handbook*, Dorling Kindersley, London, 1998.

— (edited by), *The Oxford Dictionary of World Religions*, Oxford University Press, Oxford and New York, 1997.

Brockington, J. L., *The Sacred Thread*, Edinburgh University Press, Edinburgh, 1996 (2nd Edition).

Carty, Rev. Charles Mortimer, *Padre Pio: The Stigmatist*, Tan, Rockford (Illinois), 1973.

Chopra, Deepak, *Foreword* in *The Visionary Window: A Quantum Physicist's Guide to Enlightenment* by Amit Goswami, Quest Books, Wheaton, Illinois and Chennai (Madras), 2000.

Christie-Murray, David, *Voices from the Gods: Speaking in Tongues*, Routledge and Kegan Paul, London and Henley, 1978.

Dowman, Keith, *Masters of Mahamudra: Songs and Histories of the Eighty-Four Buddhist Siddhas*, State University of New York Press, Albany, 1985.

— , *The Sacred Life of Tibet*, Thorsons, London, 1997.

Ebert, John David, *Twilight of the Clockwork Gods: Conversations on Science and Spirituality at the End of an Age*, Council Oak, Tula and San Francisco, 1999.

Eliade, Mircea, *Yoga: Immortality and Freedom*, Princeton University Press, New Jersey, 1990 (reprint).

Evans-Wentz, W. Y. (editor), *The Tibetan Book of the Dead*, Oxford University Press, Oxford, 1960 (reprint).

Farges, Albert, *Mystical Phenomena: Compared with their Human and Diabolical Counterfeits*, Burns Oates and Washbourne, London, 1926.

Feuerstein, Georg, *The Yoga-Sutras of Patanjali*, Inner Traditions International, Vermont, 1989 (reprint).

Fischer-Schreiber, Ingrid, Ehrhard, Franz-Karl, Friedrichs, Kurt and

Diener, Michael S., *The Rider Encyclopedia of Eastern Philosophy and Religion,* Rider, London, 1989.

Fox, Matthew, *The A.W.E. Project: Reinventing Education, Reinventing the Human,* CopperHouse, Kelowna, BC (Canada), 2006.

— , *Creation Spirituality: Liberating Gifts for the People of the Earth,* HarperSanFrancisco, San Francisco and New York,1991.

— , *Original Blessing: A Primer in Creation Spirituality,* Tarcher/ Putnam, New York, 2000 (reprint).

Gold, Victor Roland, Hoyt, JR., Thomas L., Ringe, Sharon H., Thistlewaite, Susan Brooks, Throckmorton, JR., Burton H., and Withers, Barbara A. (editors), *The New Testament and Psalms: An Inclusive Version,* Oxford University Press, Oxford and New York, 1995.

Gombrich, Richard F., *How Buddhism Began: The Conditioned Genesis of the Early Teachings,* Athlone, London and Atlantic Highland (New Jersey), 1996.

Goring, Rosemary (editor), *Chambers' Dictionary of Beliefs and Religions,* BCA, London, New York, Sydney, Toronto, 1992.

Govinda, Lama Anagarika, *Foundations of Tibetan Mysticism,* Rider, London, 1983 (reprint).

Griffiths, Bede, *The One Light: Bede Griffiths' Principal Writings* (edited with a commentary by Bruno Barnhart), Templegate, Springfield (Illinois), 2001.

Guiley, Rosemary Ellen, *Harper's Encyclopedia of Mystical and Paranormal Experience,* Castle Books, Edison (New Jersey), 1991.

Gunaratana, Mahathera Henepola, *The Jhanas in Theravada Buddhist Meditation,* Buddhist Publication Society, Kandy (Sri Lanka), 1988.

Hecker, Hellmuth, *Mahamoggallana: Master of Psychic Power,* chapter two in *Great Disciples of the Buddha,* by Nyanaponika and Hellmuth Hecker (edited by Bhikkhu Bodhi), Wisdom, Boston, 1997.

The Holy Bible: Today's New International Version, Hodder and

137

Stoughton, London, Sydney and Auckland, 2006 (reprint).

Jacobs, Alan (translated by), *The Gnostic Gospels: Including the Gospel of Thomas and the Gospel of Mary Magdalene*, Watkins Publishing, London, 2006.

John of the Cross, St. (translated by Kavanaugh and Rodriguez), *The Collected Works of Saint John of the Cross*, ICS, Washington, D.C., 1991 (2nd revised edition).

Jung, C. G., *Jung on the East* (edited and introduction by J. J. Clark), Routledge, London, 1995.

— , *Memories, Dreams, Reflections*, Fontana Press, London, 1995 (reprint).

King, Ursula, *Spirit of Fire: The Life and Vision of Teilhard de Chardin*, Orbis Books, New York, 1996 (5th reprint).

Krishna, Gopi, *Higher Consciousness: The Evolutionary Thrust of Kundalini,* Julian Press, New York, 1994.

Lerner, Michael, *Spirit Matters*, Walsch Books, Boston, 2000.

McKnight, Scot, *The Jesus Creed: Loving God, Loving Others* (with a foreword by John Ortberg), Paraclete Press, Brewster (Massachusetts), 2005 (4th reprint).

Malcolm, James F., *Psychic Influences in World Religion*, Spiritualists' National Union, Stansted, 1966.

Manser, Martin (compiled by), *Bible Quotation Collection*, Lion Publishing, Oxford, 1999.

Mabry, John R., *The Way of Thomas: Nine Insights for Enlightened Living from the Secret Sayings of Jesus*, O Books, Winchester and New York, 2007.

Meyer, Marvin (translated with an introduction by), *The Gospel of Thomas: The Hidden Saying of Jesus* (with an interpretation by Harold Bloom), HarperSanFrancisco, New York, 1992.

Nanamoli, Bhikkhu, *The Path of Purification: Visuddhimagga*, Buddhist Publication Society, Kandy, Sri Lanka, 1991.

Nasr, Seyyed Hossein, *Sufism and the Integration of the Inner and Outer*

Life of Man, The Temenos Academy, London 1999.

Pagels, Elaine, *Beyond Belief: The Secret Gospel of Thomas,* Pan Books, London, Basingstoke and Oxford, 2005 (3rd reprint).

Prabhavananda, Swami and Isherwood, Christopher, *How to Know God: The Yoga Aphorisms of Patanjali,* Vedanta Press, California, 1981 (reprint).

Primack, Joel and Abrams, Nancy Ellen, *The View from the Centre of the Universe: Discovering our Extraordinary Place in the Cosmos,* Fourth Estate, London, 2006.

Rama, Swami, *Living with the Himalayan Masters,* Himilayan Institute, Honesdale, 1978 (revised edition).

Redfield, James, *The Celestine Prophecy: An Adventure,* Warner Books, New York, 1994.

Rukmani, T. S., *Siddhis in the Bhagavata Purana and in the Yogasutras of Patanjali: A Comparison,* chapter sixteen in *Researches in Indian and Buddhist Philosophy: Essays in Honour of Prof. Alex Wayman* (edited by Ram Karan Sharma), Montilal Banarsidass, Delhi, 1993.

Santoshan, *The Miraculous Self,* appendix two in *The House of Wisdom: Yoga Spirituality of the East and West,* by Dharmananda, Swami and Santoshan, O Books, Winchester and New York, 2007.

Schimmel, Annemarie, *Mystical Dimensions of Islam,* The University of North Carolina Press, Chapel Hill, 1978 (3rd edition).

Schmidt, Roger, *Exploring Religion,* Wadsworth, Belmont (California), 1988 (2nd Edition).

Schucman, Helen, *A Course in Miracles: Text, Workbook for Students and Manual for Teachers,* Foundation for Inner Peace, Hill Valley (California), 1992 (2nd edition).

Skorupski, Tadeusz, *The Religions of Tibet,* chapter twelve in *The World's Religions: The Religions of Asia* (edited by Friedhelm Hardy), Routledge, London, 1990 (reprint).

Staal, Frits, *Exploring Mysticism: A Methodological Approach,* University of California Press, California, 1975.

Teresa, St., *The Life of Saint Teresa by Herself,* Penguin, London, 1959.

Thittila, Maha Thera U., *The Fundamental Principles of Theravada Buddhism,* chapter 2 in *The Path of the Buddha: Buddhism interpreted by Buddhists* (edited by Kenneth Morgan), Montilal Banarsidass, Delhi, 1993 (reprint).

Thurston, Herbert S. J. (edited by J.H. Crehan), *The Physical Phenomena of Mysticism,* Burns Oates, London, 1952.

Underhill, Evelyn, *Mysticism: A Study in the Nature and Development in Man's Spiritual Consciousness,* Methuen and Co. Ltd., London, 1930 (12th revised edition).

Vogl, Adalbert Albert, *Therese Neumann: Mystic and Stigmatist, 1898-1962,* Tan Books, Rockford (Illinios), 1987.

Waida, Manabu, *Miracles,* article in *The Encyclopedia of Religion: Vol. 9* (edited by Mircea Eliade), Macmillan, New York and London, 1987.

Woods, James Haughton, *The Yoga-System of Patanjali: Or the Ancient Hindu Doctrine of Concentration of Mind,* Motilal Banarsidass, Delhi, 1992 (reprint).

Yogananda, Paramahansa, *Autobiography of a Yogi,* Self-Realization Fellowship, California, 1993 (12th reprint).

Website references (October 2007)
allexperts.com/q/Hindus-946/Miracles-Krishna.htm
boltwolf.tripod.com/id119.html
iqra.net/Hadith/miracle.php
menorah.org/starofdavid.html
mohammad-pbuh.com/3/othermiracles.htm
parami.org/buddhistanswers/what_about_miracles.htm
sunnahonline.com/ilm/seerah/0083.htm
wikipedia.org/wiki/Bible_prophecy
wikipedia.org/wiki/Muhammad#Seal_of_the_prophets

The Gordon Higginson Fellowship formed for the purpose of launching an integral spiritual organisation that allows for diversity in belief, and would continuously explore crucial facets of individual, social and global spirituality and creative avenues of transpersonal phenomena.

Mission Statement
To share the truth of an eternal spiritual existence and grow towards embodying its greatest wisdom.

NINE UNFOLDMENTS

1. To awaken to the oneness of the Supreme Self and the immanent and transcendent Divine universe.

Thread of meaning: Behind the appearance of individuality there is an ultimate interconnectedness that permeates all – a Divinity that works and is universally present within our cosmos and also transcends it. There are numerous successive ways, openings and various centring levels of being through which this Truth can be realised and experienced, such as moments in nature and meditative states of awareness, through worship, forms of prayer, creative abilities and everyday acts of kindness.

2. To find unity with and realise the sacredness of all existence.

Thread of meaning: Life is unique, precious and sacred. As humans we belong to one global family and need to use our Divine gifts to find ways of becoming co-creators and overcome the boundaries that separate and stop us from caring for each other, as well as cherishing and protecting the earth and life upon it.

3. To explore wider states of consciousness and creative uses of transpersonal insight.

Thread of meaning: The transpersonal realm, which houses states of awareness beyond the restraints of personal identity, is interwoven with the collective unconscious mind. In the emergence of spiritual development, transcendent, transformative and unconscious influences can be revealed through various practices. Meditative, shamanistic, mystical and superconscious intuitive experiences all function through this level in an expansive number of ways and, if integrated correctly, they can help us become aware of the spirit's existence and the infinite qualities of good within us.

4. To cultivate wholesome awareness and skilful use of the will.

Thread of meaning: Growth involves expanding our awareness in an ongoing healthy direction that helps us embody a balanced life. To find peace in our being and establish it in the communities in which we live, our actions and thoughts require elements of mindfulness, patience, wisdom and openness.

5. To harmonise one's life and transcend the individual I-consciousness.

Thread of meaning: All areas and facets of our life – the physical, emotional, mental and spiritual – function more naturally when they are in tune with one another and harmonised into a complete whole. In the nurturing of spiritual growth our individual sense of 'I', which often seeks to protect itself and be favoured over others, will need to learn how to let life in securely before moving on to integrate all-embracing selfless states of being and uncovering unitive levels of consciousness. A healthy 'I' is therefore part of development.

6. To purify the mind and heart, and perform wise and compassionate actions.

Thread of meaning: The emotions and the mind are two essential areas that require exploration to see how they can become more wholesome, open to accepting others and spiritually engaged in life in skilful ways.

7. To attain selfless freedom in everyday living and activities.

Thread of meaning: By being in the present moment, cultivating congruent, deep and meaningful relationships with all and transforming inhibiting patterns of thought, action and reaction, we find liberation, creative interaction and spontaneousness, and more authentic realms of existence, love and awareness.

8. To honour the great wisdom traditions and be open to new truths and knowledge.

Thread of meaning: There are treasures in all the great traditions which can help us live a spiritually centred life. We also live in multi-cultural societies and are surrounded by people from different faiths. If we do not seek to understand our global neighbours, look for common ground and accept diversity, then we will never find lasting peace in the world or our development, as true growth does not imply only living in harmony with those who think the same as us. Equally, we need to be receptive to contemporary knowledge that widens our perceptions about life within and around us.

9. To grow continuously in the spiritual search and have joy in other people's accomplishments.

Thread of meaning: Authentic growth is not self-centred, but an ongoing organic process that continuously expands to encompass all as a profound spiritual synthesis. When our development includes others, we open to the richness of their wisdom, goodness and creativity.

HELP TO SUPPORT THE GHF

If you would like to help to sponsor the Gordon Higginson
Fellowship to publish further titles and promote its teachings,
or purchace further books, please write to
Santoshan, c/o 33 Cobden Road, London E11 3PE
e-mail santoshan@ghf-web.com

**For information about the Fellowship and courses visit
www.ghf-web.com**

FELLOWSHIP SYMBOL

Double Circle
The omnipresent and
transcendent nature of the Divine.
The circle is also a universal symbol
of wholeness and unity.

Triangle
A double meaning of the seeker's
quest and Divine inspiration.

4 Segments
(1) Love
(2) Selfless work
(3) Wise discernment
(4) Transpersonal knowledge

Note
The circle, triangle and oblong
are the three basic shapes in
Creation.